THE ITALIANS IN OKLAHOMA

By Kenny L. Brown

Oklahoma Image is a project sponsored by the
Oklahoma Department of Libraries
and the Oklahoma Library Association,
and made possible by a grant from the
National Endowment for the Humanities.

Library of Congress Cataloging in Publication Data

Brown, Kenny L.
  The Italians in Oklahoma

  (Newcomers to a new land)
  Bibliography: p.
  1. Italian Americans — Oklahoma — History.   2. Oklahoma —
History.   I. Title.   II. Series.
F705.I8B76   976.6'004'51   79-23342

ISBN 978-0-8061-1624-2 (paper)

CONTENTS

For Diane and Stephanie

PREFACE

This short history of the Italians in Oklahoma is written for the general reader—it is designed to be both enjoyable and informative. If this work offers anything to the specialist, it is two observations concerning the Italian experience in the Sooner State. First, it describes the virtually complete assimilation of the Italian in Oklahoma. In past years, students of immigration have debated this issue. Much of the recent evidence indicates that assimilation was limited and incomplete in urban areas. There various immigrant groups have isolated and separated themselves from the general population. But some writers have indicated that the absorption into the general society was virtually complete in rural areas and small towns. This was the case for the Italians of Oklahoma. This study also points out the unique situations and problems that the Italians encountered in Oklahoma. Before statehood in Indian Territory they faced legal restrictions and certain hardships not found elsewhere.

Because more Italians settled in the coal-mining district than in any other place, the bulk of this work deals with that region. In particular, Coal, Latimer, Okmulgee, and Pittsburg counties are emphasized because they had the largest Italian populations. Likewise the mining town of Krebs is often discussed because of its large Italian population, approaching what might be called a "colony." This study also focuses on the time period from approximately 1890 to the mid 1920s when the Italian immigrants had their greatest impact. Often the census data from 1910 is most frequently cited because it was a watershed year for immigration as reflected in the census statistics.

Some of the material within this booklet appeared earlier in the article "Peaceful Progress: A History of the Italians of Krebs, Oklahoma," *The Chronicles of Oklahoma* 53 (Fall 1975): 332–52. It is reprinted with the permission of the Oklahoma Historical Society.

Many people helped in numerous ways in the completion of this study. Thanks is particularly extended to several Italians of various generations who gave much valuable information. Those who allowed extensive interviews were: John Marino, Sr., Bill Prichard, Carmine and Maria Finamore, and Santi and Minnie Cioni, all from Krebs; Albert Messina and Bert Tua from McAlester; Tony Ravaioli from Haileyville; Ed Menghini and Martina Dufour from Coalgate; Minnie Appling and Romeo Battalio from Wilburton; Jim Palesano from Anadarko; and Mike Caruso, Sr., from Fort Cobb. Special acknowledgment is given to three men, now deceased, who gave enormously valuable information in their interviews: Pete Echelle of Kiowa, Dominic Rossi of Krebs, and Charles Fassino of McAlester.

An additional debt of gratitude is owed to two teachers in the history department at Oklahoma State University, who periodically encouraged and guided me on this endeavor. Dr. Norbert Mahnken aided me not only on this project but also helped foster an interest in and love for Oklahoma history. Dr. Douglas Hale, who directed me toward the study of Italians in Oklahoma, always provided encouragement and advice as well as a brilliant example to follow. Finally, my wife, Diane, deserves much praise and thanks for her tolerance and constructive help in finishing this history. It is to her and my daughter, Stephanie, that I dedicate this work.

Panhandle State University   *Kenny L. Brown*

Chapter 1

THE ITALIAN BACKGROUND

In 1905 Adolfo Rossi, an official from Italy's Royal Emigration Department, visited Krebs and McAlester, Oklahoma, on his tour of the United States. At those two towns he found several hundred Italians working in the coal mines nearby. With the pay so good, about $2.50 per day, these immigrants had few complaints or problems. They frugally saved their earnings and, distrusting banks, buried them underground. Some donated money for a new church for their old village back in Italy. A few, according to Rossi, operated grocery stores and other businesses; two Italian brothers even owned a macaroni factory in McAlester. Almost all ate well, and had home gardens. Rossi noted only one complaint from the Italians: they could have no alcoholic beverages in Indian Territory.

In general, most of the conditions that Rossi found in McAlester and Krebs resembled those experienced by his countrymen whom he visited in other parts of the country. Nonetheless, the lives of the Italians in Indian Territory, and later Oklahoma, were in some ways unique and in many ways significant. Because of the unusual governmental situation in Indian Territory, they faced hardships and restrictions on their customs not encountered by their compatriots in other locations in the United States. Despite these obstacles the Italians of Oklahoma, like those in the American West and in other rural areas, eventually assimilated into the society of the region.[1] In addition, these Italian immigrants, along with other non-Indians in Oklahoma, contributed significantly to the state's economic development. Concentrated in the coal-mining communities, they also had a strong impact on the variety and color of the society in the area. The story of the Italians in Oklahoma is a significant part of immigration history as well as a colorful part of the state's past.

The Italians coming to Oklahoma made up only a small portion of the enormous population that left Italy at the same time. There were several reasons for that mass exodus. When considering the glory and attractiveness of Italy's ancient, medieval, and Renaissance past, the explanation is not abundantly clear. After all, their homeland was the center of power and control of the known world during the days when Rome dominated the Mediterranean area. Even during the Middle Ages, Italy continued to be important with Rome as the center for religious authority throughout most of western Europe. During the Renaissance the city-states of Italy led the globe economically, scientifically, and culturally as Europe revived as the focus of world power. What explained the mass migration from an area with such a splendid past? The answers lay in the developments that created unbearable economic conditions for many Italians in the late nineteenth and early twentieth centuries.

During the 1500s the focus of cultural and financial activities switched from Italy to England, France, Spain, and other countries on the Atlantic. These western European nations surpassed Italy because of the discovery of North America, which made their position more favorable for world trade. They were unified under strong central governments, a situation advantageous to economic growth. Italy remained only a geographic expression composed of several small competitive kingdoms. Spain, Austria, and France invaded and controlled much of the peninsula throughout the many decades that followed. The substandard national and economic development during this era caused Italy to fall far behind other countries.

Eventually the democratic philosophies nurtured by the Enlightenment of the eighteenth century appealed to a few Italians of the middle and upper classes. They associated the unification of their country with republican ideals. This small philosophical beginning ironically was bolstered with the invasion and control of Italy under Napoleon between 1796 and 1814. During that period the French unified for the first time in centuries much of the central and northern sections of the peninsula. Even the south indirectly fell under the control of Napoleon's designs. Although subjugated, Italy experienced administrative, economic, and political unification. After Napoleon's defeat in 1814, the region lapsed into its previous state of fragmentation.

Even with its negative effects, the French domination kindled a nationalist movement. The Italian merchants and middle class, who grew prosperous under the Napoleonic rule, realized the economic advantages of a unified state. Others became weary of foreign control and wished to oust all outsiders. The democratic idealists still yearned for freedom. These radicals, along with the nationalists and merchants, formed the leadership for the unification movement between 1814 and 1870, a period known as the *Risorgimento*.[2]

Probably the most influential of those who struggled in this complex formation of the country were the leaders of the new commercial classes. They realized, if the small countries located on or near the peninsula were combined into one nation, tariffs and taxes could be eliminated or reduced. A centralized government could also provide roads and railways for transporting goods. Many future-oriented Italians excitedly anticipated the possibilities of a new Suez canal. If the region could unify politically and economically, the country could then take advantage of its position to gain control of the commerce created by a new canal. Italy could even become the center of world trade again.

The less profit-minded republicans had other motivations. Many of their ideas came from the writings and speeches of Giuseppe Mazzini. Often in exile, Mazzini worked to instigate a general insurrection to unify Italy as a democratic republic. He advocated radical measures such as social and economic equality for the suppressed peasants at the expense of the ruling class. Other writers and philosophers added to the unification movement by giving Italians a consciousness of nationalism and romanticism similar to the ideas then sweeping the rest of Europe in the early nineteenth century.

The various economic, nationalistic, and republican catalysts culminated in attempts to overthrow the despotic rulers in several areas in order to unify the various units into one nation. The most spectacular of these unsuccessful attempts was the revolution of 1848–49, when Piedmont led various other areas in a fleeting attempt to create one Italy.

The major obstacle to the formation of the Italian nation in these early stages was the failure of any one of the small kingdoms to become powerful enough to lead the movement. Some realized that outside help might be necessary, particularly in ousting the Austrians from the northern region and then keeping them from interfering with subsequent unification. Ultimately Piedmont provided the needed strength and leadership under its prime minister, Camillo Benso di Cavour. In 1859 and 1860 Cavour used an alliance with the French emperor Napoleon III to oust the Austrians and to support the assimilation of much of Italy into one country. At the same time, he took advantage of Giuseppe Garibaldi's exploits in southern Italy by send-

3

ing the Piedmontese army to take possession of lands that Garibaldi liberated. At the end of 1860 only Venetia and the province surrounding Rome remained outside the new country, and by 1870 those areas were also incorporated as part of the nation.

The unified Italy that resulted from the leadership of Cavour was not the utopia that many of the revolutionaries had wanted. Cavour had supported change but was moderate or even conservative in his approach. He feared that a complete break with tradition would be disastrous and fashioned the new government into a monarchy. Victor Emmanuel II, originally the ruler of Piedmont, became the King of Italy with a strong control over the ministers and parliament. In the years that followed unification, the conservatism of the government persisted, and the country changed only gradually. The fragile unification made the leaders more concerned about holding the country together than addressing new social and political issues. Often they answered dissension and insurrection with authoritarianism and armed force, while they ignored the complex problems that had actually created the difficulties. As governmental leadership changed later in the nineteenth century, some officials attempted to correct the situation; yet others, caught up in faddish imperialism, spent much of their energy trying to create a colonial empire. The result was a stagnant economy and a calamitous social atmosphere that caused a mass exodus from the country.[3]

A major problem leading to emigration was inequitable land ownership. The control of land by a select few had been established under the feudal system in medieval times when only nobility could own land. Italians were slow to change this situation and actually never fully outgrew the practice. In the eighteenth century in Tuscany and Sardinia, leaders attempted some reforms when they broke up a few large estates and sold them to peasants, but most of this land eventually reverted to the large landholders. Following the invasion by Napoleon, feudalism generally was abolished; unfortunately the obligations and responsibilities of the landlords also vanished. Peasants could buy land, but, as with the earlier attempts, the land returned to large landowners because of the peasants' financial inability to run the farms.

After unification, a new middle class of landed gentry and merchants successfully challenged the old nobility for a prominent position in society. These new leaders, however, were only a small portion of the population, and the masses continued to consist of poor peasants. In the early years of nationhood the government again at-

4

tempted reform as church lands and communally owned plots were auctioned off with the hope of providing better distribution. In addition, many peasants bought other private lands. The poor quality of the soil and the harsh taxation of the new government overburdened the small farmers, forcing them once again to sell. The number of persons owning property actually declined between 1861 and 1901, and the control by the large proprietors continued. In southern Italy the *latifundi,* or large plantation-like farms, predominated and most farmers were simply day laborers. The *mezzadria* system, or share-cropping, became the usual mode of agriculture in central Italy. Farming in northern Italy also involved large holdings, but there the plight of the peasant was lessened somewhat by the growth of industry.

A related socioeconomic problem in Italy was the "southern question" involving economic conditions in seven regions: Abruzzi, Campania, Molise, Puglia, Basilicata, Calabria, and Sicily. At the time the nation was formed, these areas were much less developed than those in northern Italy. In subsequent years the situation worsened as the economy of the south fell far behind that of the areas to the north. In southern Italy this developed from strong dependency on an agriculture that progressed very slowly. The area had a scarcity of water and mineral resources as well as transportation problems that retarded the development of industry. Conditions in northern Italy, although not ideal, allowed that region to prosper to a much greater degree. The north had a better supply of raw materials, fairly adequate transportation, and a location near the more industrialized countries.

The social and political disparities were probably the most distressing aspects of the southern question. From the beginning, the people in the south became so troublesome that troops were sent from the north to occupy the area and prevent revolt. The southerners resisted the intrusion of northern control. Because many of the leaders of unification came from the north, representatives of that region continued to exert dominant governmental influence. These politicians often supported legislation that aided the industrial north at the expense of the agricultural south. In the 1880s Italy passed tariffs designed to protect industry. This provoked a retaliatory trade war with France, and agriculture, particularly in the south, suffered. Even more unfair were the disproportionate tax rates charged in the south. The literacy rate was lower and the poverty rate higher in the south. Crime and corruption became famous in this area with the formation of extralegal groups such as the *mafia* in Sicily and the *camorra* in Naples.

Citizens in the north sometimes explained these differences by declaring or implying that southern Italians were racially degenerate —a belief that continued into the twentieth century. More liberal northerners with even milder prejudices regarded the southerners as lazy and an impediment to progress. In rebuttal, southerners often claimed that self-seeking groups in the north had caused the problems by making high profits and blocking progress in the south. These social attitudes, the political imbalance, and, most important of all, the poor economic conditions led to a mass emigration from the south between 1906 and 1913. In this period, approximately one-half of Italy's emigrants came from that region.

Another problem strongly affecting Italy was the constant general stagnation of the economy. Both agricultural and industrial pursuits failed to prosper, causing hundreds of Italians to seek better conditions in foreign countries. During the second half of the nineteenth century, farming techniques and equipment improved, but most of Italy's agricultural population remained at the subsistence level

A typical scene in Italy at Giaveno, near Turin, about 1920. Maria Ferrando, seated at the table, had relatives living in Alderson, Oklahoma. Courtesy of Mrs. Edith Hamilton.

ITALY

Trentino

Lombardia

Veneto

Friuli-
Venezia Giulia

Piemonte

Liguria

Emilia-Romagna

Toscana

Marche

Umbria

Lazio

Abruzzi

Molise

Campania

Puglia

Basilicata

SARDINIA

Calabria

SICILY

25 0 25 50 75

Miles

N

throughout the period. The most basic problem was the scarcity of good farm land in this largely mountainous country that was only half arable. Conditions were particularly dismal from 1874 to 1896 during the prolonged national depression that caused many people to lose their farms. Even though limited prosperity eventually developed, after 1900 certain types of farmers periodically experienced disasters. In 1903 phylloxera destroyed many of the vineyards, while crop failures and falling prices also created an intolerable situation that led to emigration. The poor peasant farmers who constituted one-half the population barely produced sufficient food for their families. Bread, wine, minestrone, and a little meat made up the average diet. Farm dwellings were so inadequate that peasant families often slept with animals for warmth in the winter.

As in agriculture, progress in industry came very slowly and incompletely to Italy and helped lead to a mass migration from the country. Local industrial expansion occurred between 1896 and 1908 in the northern areas of Lombardy, Tuscany, Liguria, and Piedmont; however, the growth was not sufficient to support the unemployed who were flooding the cities from the agricultural regions. Urban living conditions were only slightly better than those on the land. The industrial worker labored twelve to fourteen hours a day and went home to a dwelling that by American standards would have been called a shack.

While social inequities and the economic retardation in Italy discouraged many of its citizens, overpopulation further increased pressure on the people. Between 1871 and 1905 the number of Italians increased by 25 percent despite a large emigration; the population density increased from 257 per square mile to 294. Large-scale emigration was understandable. More than twenty-five million people left Italy in its first hundred years of existence as a nation.

Initially, the migration of Italians was internal with large numbers leaving the agricultural areas and settling in the cities. The first emigration consisted of northern Italians going to neighboring European countries; most of these returned after a short stay. This pattern of migration changed in the 1880s and 1890s with the exodus of southern Italians from Basilicata, Calabria, Campania, Abruzzi, and Sicily. The initial flow of transoceanic emigration went first to Brazil and Argentina, but by the late 1890s a much larger number of Italians, mostly from the south, were going to the United States. Although the majority of these returned home, they tended to stay abroad more permanently than their northern compatriots who went to

European countries. The exodus from Italy which started as a trickle, developed into a flood of people by 1900. The annual out-migration between 1861 and 1870 was 121,040. Between 1901 and 1910, the average was 602,669. Thereafter the number dropped significantly.

Migration from Italy followed discernible patterns. Approximately four-fifths of the emigrants were males between twenty and fifty years of age. Many of these men went first, then sent for their wives or women they wanted to marry. Only after 1887 did whole families go abroad together, though the tendency for men to go alone still predominated. Occasionally almost entire populations of some villages traveled to America; a few of the hamlets in the more remote districts of Italy retained a population of only old men, women, and children. In 1902, Prime Minister Giuseppe Zanardelli made a trip through southern Italy and was shocked by the mayor of Moliterno who greeted him "on behalf of the eight thousand people in this commune, three thousand of whom are in America and the other five thousand preparing to follow them."[4]

The Italians who came to the United States were part of the great historical epic of immigration. During the early and middle nineteenth century thousands of foreigners entered the country, the large majority of these coming from the British Isles and western and northern Europe. In the late nineteenth and early twentieth centuries, the trend changed as millions of southern and eastern Europeans immigrated, coming from Russia, Austria-Hungary, and Italy. Generally uneducated and with strange languages and customs, these people came in large numbers and were only gradually assimilated into American society.[5]

By 1920 the total migration from Italy to the United States was 4,195,880. This influx into the United States started very slowly; for example, only 12,354 entered in 1880. The amount increased significantly after 1900, the top years being 1907 with 285,731 and 1914 with 283,738. Although the number of newcomers was great, over half returned to their homeland. Those who remained congregated primarily in the urban areas of New York and neighboring states. The 1900 census indicated that a majority of the Italians lived in cities with more than 25,000 inhabitants. In 1910 the average Italian entering the United States had only about seventeen dollars in his pocket. It was necessary for him to accept the first employment available in the metropolitan areas of the Northeast. However, many Italians had made arrangements with friends or relatives to locate in other parts of the country where their compatriots were already established. Seeking the highest paying jobs, thousands went to various areas in the United States to work on construction projects, in industries, on railroads, as ditchdiggers, and in mines—including the coal mines in Oklahoma.

Table I

IMMIGRATION TO THE UNITED STATES
FROM ITALY, BY YEAR, 1880-1920

1880 = 12,354	1901 = 135,996
1881 = 15,401	1902 = 178,375
1882 = 32,159	1903 = 230,622
1883 = 31,792	1904 = 193,296
1884 = 16,510	1905 = 221,479
1885 = 13,642	1906 = 273,120
1886 = 21,315	1907 = 285,731
1887 = 47,622	1908 = 128,503
1888 = 51,558	1909 = 183,218
1889 = 25,307	1910 = 215,537
1890 = 52,003	1911 = 182,882
1891 = 76,055	1912 = 157,134
1892 = 61,631	1913 = 265,542
1893 = 72,145	1914 = 283,738
1894 = 42,977	1915 = 49,688
1895 = 35,427	1916 = 33,665
1896 = 68,060	1917 = 34,596
1897 = 59,431	1918 = 5,250
1898 = 58,613	1919 = 1,884
1899 = 77,419	1920 = 95,145
1900 = 100,135	

Source: U.S., Bureau of the Census, *Historical Statistics of the United States, Colonial Times to 1957* (Washington, D.C.: Government Printing Office, 1957), pp. 56–57.

Table II

NUMBER OF PERMANENT ITALIAN-BORN SETTLERS
COMPARED WITH TOTAL NUMBER
OF ITALIAN IMMIGRANTS

Permanent Settlers	Total Immigrants
1860 = 11,677	1860 = 13,793
1870 = 17,157	1870 = 25,518
1880 = 44,230	1880 = 81,277
1890 = 182,580	1890 = 388,586
1900 = 484,027	1900 = 1,040,479
1910 = 1,343,125	1910 = 3,086,356
1920 = 1,610,113	1920 = 4,195,880

Source: U.S., Bureau of the Census, *Historical Statistics of the United States, Colonial Times to 1957* (Washington, D.C.: Government Printing Office, 1957), pp. 56–57, 66.

Chapter 2

ITALIAN IMMIGRATION TO OKLAHOMA

In comparison to more than four million Italians who migrated to the United States by 1920, Oklahoma's Italian population seems small. In 1910, the peak year, 2,564 Italians lived in the state.[1] Among the twenty-two states west of the Mississippi River, Oklahoma ranked fifteenth. Oklahoma's Italian population, however, was highly concentrated with 85 percent living in the coal-mining communities of the southeastern section. This compact distribution caused the Italians of Oklahoma to have a surprisingly strong impact on the economy and society of the communities where they lived.

The coal deposits of Oklahoma that attracted the Italian immigrants were not first developed until the 1870s. Governmental officials had known of coal deposits in the area as early as the 1830s when the Five Civilized Tribes were relocated in Indian Territory. The first white man to take advantage of these resources was James J. McAlester, owner of a general store at the juncture of the Texas Road and the California Trail in the Choctaw Nation. McAlester came to the area because he had read a geologist's notebook that indicated the richest deposits of coal lay near the Crossroads. In 1872 he took a wagonload of this top-grade bituminous coal to officials of the Missouri, Kansas, and Texas Railroad at Parsons, Kansas. The high quality of the coal and McAlester's persuasion induced the officials to develop the coal resources around the settlement that later became McAlester. The Missouri, Kansas, and Texas Railroad was the first customer for Oklahoma coal; eventually, this railroad and others owned most of the mines in the area.[2]

Although the first coal mines in Indian Territory opened near McAlester in 1872, later major operations moved eastward after the establishment of a camp at Krebs in 1875. Other communities soon developed with the building of new railroads throughout the coal-

12

mining district. By the 1880s the pattern followed two directions from the original McAlester-Krebs area. To the east along the Choctaw, Oklahoma, and Gulf Railroad were Alderson, Hartshorne, and Wilburton. To the southwest along the Missouri, Kansas, and Texas Railroad were Savanna, Coalgate, and Lehigh. Located in present-day Pittsburg, Coal, and Latimer counties, these communities and numerous other smaller nearby mining camps became the core of intensive coal production. In the 1890s and early 1900s additional areas in Okmulgee, LeFlore, and Haskell counties opened to production. There were smaller operations, mostly strip mines, in the vicinity of Ardmore, near Tulsa, and just west of the M. K. & T. Railroad between Muskogee and Vinita.

The labor supply was a problem in these areas from the beginning. Few white men lived in Indian Territory, and the Choctaw Indians were not enthusiastic about mining. As a result, company agents went to other coalfields in the United States to recruit miners, most of whom were immigrants. In 1873 and 1874 the first workers were brought in, mostly from Pennsylvania, comprised of Americans, English, Irish, Scots, and Welshmen. A few southern and eastern Europeans, including Italians, also arrived with some of the early groups, but they were small in number. Initially, the English-speaking miners grew discouraged by the living conditions in this frontier area because there were no towns or cities. The owners of the mines also disliked the English-speaking miners because they supported the labor movement; therefore southern and eastern Europeans were brought into the area in increasing numbers as the mines developed. Mine operators paid some of the early immigrants to visit their homelands and persuade friends to return with them under contract to work in the coalfields of Indian Territory, but the majority of the early foreigners came from the other mining areas of the United States.

Oklahoma had a small alien population of only 2.1 percent during the height of immigration in the early twentieth century; however, in the mining region and in a few other areas, foreigners made up a large portion of the population. In 1910 three major coal producing counties had the largest percentages of foreign-born population in the state—Coal (10 percent), Latimer (7.8 percent), and Pittsburg (7.1 percent). The population of these three counties averaged 17 percent foreign stock (foreign born, native born with both parents born in a foreign country, and native born of mixed parentage). Okmulgee County, a fourth county important in coal mining, had only 2.1 percent in 1910, but by 1920 the numbers of foreign born increased in this county where coal mining developed late. The immigrants throughout the four counties totaled 6,270 in 1910, and primarily consisted of natives of the British Isles, Russia, Poland, Germany, Lithuania, Mexico and Italy. The largest single group was from Italy. The first Italians entered the region in 1875, and two or three hundred were in the vicinity in 1883. Thereafter they increased in number. Over 2,200 foreign-born Italians populated the four major coal-producing counties in 1910, totaling about one-third of the total foreign-born population in the area.

Pittsburg County claimed the largest number of all immigrants in the coal-producing area and the second highest in the state with 3,367 listed in 1910. Of these foreign-born residents the Italians were by far the largest single nationality, numbering 1,398. The principal Italian colony in the county, as well as in the state, was in Krebs. Originally a small mining camp inhabited by English and Irish, Krebs was founded about 1874. At the peak of immigration in 1910 Krebs had more foreign-born settlers than any town over 2,500 in population except Muskogee and Oklahoma City. Its 33.7 percent foreign born and 66.3 percent foreign stock surpassed all towns of above 2,500 in 1910.

Most of the immigrants in Krebs were Italians. They first arrived in 1875, and more continued to settle there as the mines prospered. As with other mining towns, the Italian population continually fluctuated in Krebs. In 1911, the Senate-sponsored Immigration Commission estimated that the population of the town and the adjacent area was about 3,000 of which 1,100 were foreign-born Italians or their children. A few Lithuanians, Poles, Syrians, and other immigrants also inhabited Krebs during the same time period.

McAlester also had an important Italian population. There, small groups of Italians inhabited many of the company houses near the mines located in what was called "North" McAlester. Many of these left the town when larger mines opened to the east. Other important communities with varying numbers of Italians were Haileyville, Hartshorne, Alderson, Dow, Archibald, Richville, and Pittsburg. The continually mobile Italian population could be found in almost every other mining town in the county.

Coal County ranked second in the number of Italian settlers. Lehigh, established in 1880, was the first coal camp in that county. Mine owners moved the site several times, eventually locating the permanent town in 1884. Two years later Coalgate was founded.

NUMBER OF OKLAHOMA RESIDENTS
BORN IN ITALY, BY COUNTY

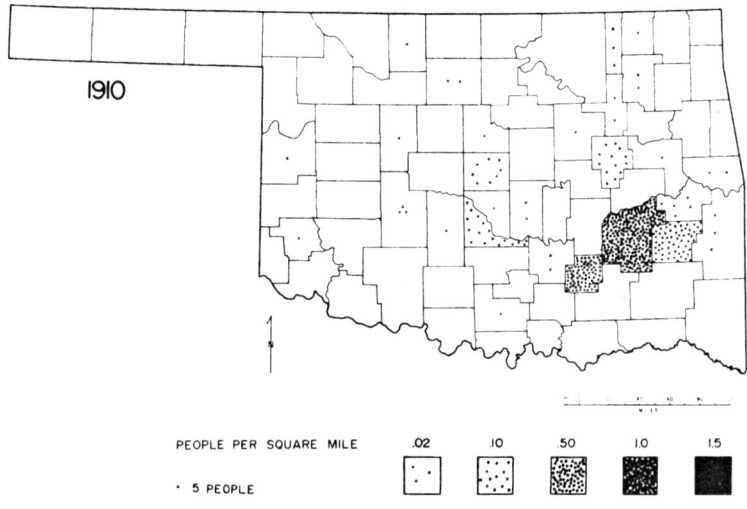

1910

PEOPLE PER SQUARE MILE   .02   .10   .50   1.0   1.5

· 5 PEOPLE

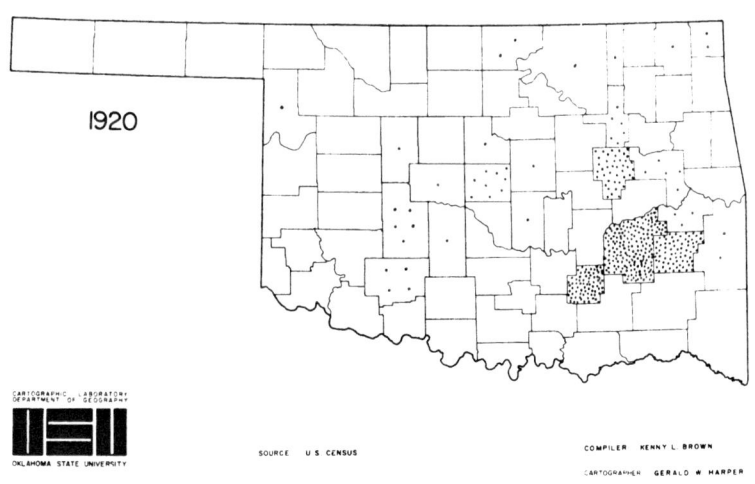

1920

CARTOGRAPHIC LABORATORY
DEPARTMENT OF GEOGRAPHY

OKLAHOMA STATE UNIVERSITY

SOURCE   U.S. CENSUS

COMPILER   KENNY L. BROWN

CARTOGRAPHER   GERALD W HARPER

Courtesy of Douglas Hale and the *Chronicles of Oklahoma.*

The Italians in Oklahoma

Although not as dominant as in Krebs, the population of the foreign stock included 1,206 out of 3,255. Other nearby towns such as Phillips and Midway soon developed. As in Pittsburg County, Italians were the largest group, numbering 443. Along with the second generation and several undesignated Italians from the old Austrian Tyrol, approximately 700 lived in the county.

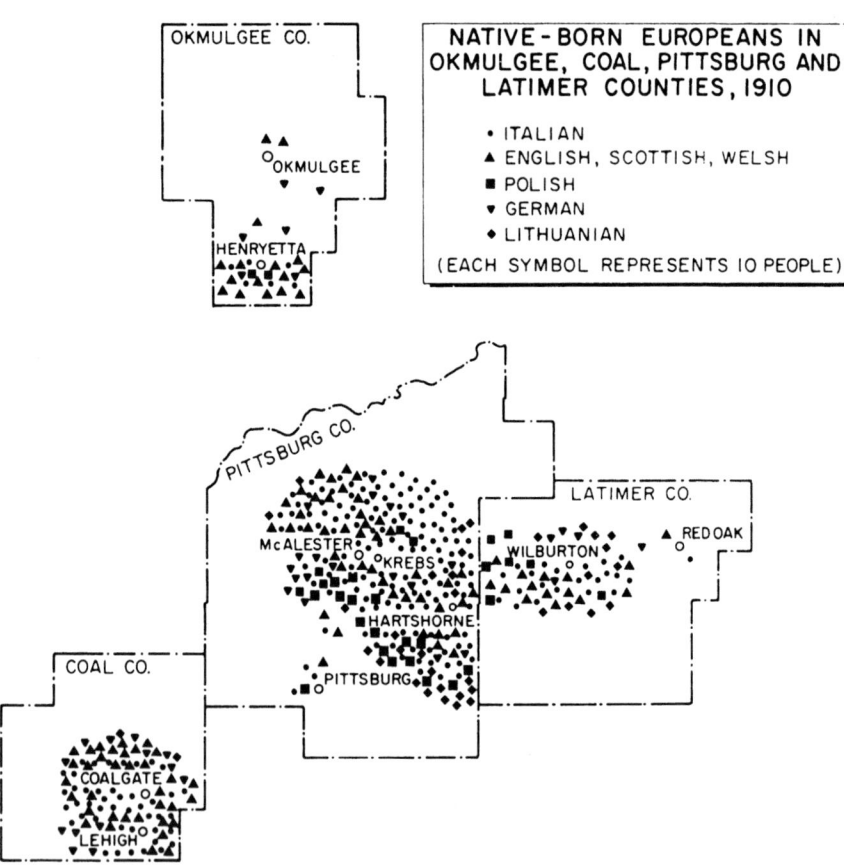

Courtesy of Douglas Hale and the *Chronicles of Oklahoma.*

Table III
FOREIGN-BORN POPULATION IN PRINCIPAL COAL-MINING COUNTIES, 1910

	Total Population	Total Foreign Born White	Percent Foreign Born White	Native Born Foreign Or Mixed Parentage	Total Foreign Stock	Percent Foreign Stock
Coal	15,817	1,575	10.0	1,656	3,231	20.4
Latimer	11,321	879	7.8	843	1,722	15.2
Okmulgee	21,115	449	2.1	768	1,217	5.8
Pittsburg	47,650	3,367	7.1	3,877	7,244	15.2

Source: United States Bureau of the Census, *Thirteenth Census of the United States taken in the year 1910*, Vol. III: *Population* (11 Vols., Washington: Government Printing Office, 1913), pp. 468, 472, 476.

Table IV
ITALIANS IN PRINCIPAL COAL-MINING COUNTIES, 1910

	Total Foreign Born White	Foreign Born Italians	Percent Italian of Total Foreign Born	Native Born With Both Parents Italian	Total Foreign Born Italians & Native Born With Both Parents Italian
Coal	1,575	443	28.1	223	666
Latimer	879	321	36.5	97	418
Okmulgee	449	64	14.3	20	84
Pittsburg	3,367	1,398	41.5	840	2,238
Total	6,270	2,226	35.5	1,180	3,406

Source: United States Bureau of the Census, *Thirteenth Census of the United States taken in the year 1910*, Vol. III: *Population* (11 Vols., Washington: Government Printing Office, 1913), pp. 468, 472, 476.

In Latimer County 321 Italians inhabited the coal-mining towns in 1910. Ranking third in the number of foreign-born Italians, this county also included about 100 of the second generation. Coal mines first opened in the county in the late 1880s with Wilburton as the principal town. Approximately half of the Italians in the county lived in that town, but large numbers also lived in Lutie, a small mining camp to the east. Others lived at Gowen, Red Oak, Hughes, and additional communities.

Coal mining developed much later in Okmulgee County, which had only sixty-four Italians in 1910. However, by 1920, 209 lived there. The first mines opened near Henryetta in 1900 when a subsidiary of the St. Louis and San Francisco Railroad was built through the region. Full-scale development did not occur until the period between 1903 and 1915, and with it came the establishment of other small mining camps such as Dewar, Bryant, Coalton, and Schulter. Coal mine operators brought in one of the first groups of Italians in 1903 when they imported about fifty from the coalfields in Indiana. Additional Italian miners drifted into the area between 1910 and 1920.[3]

The Italians in Oklahoma came from virtually every region of Italy. Starting in 1875, a majority were northern Italians from Piedmont and Venetia. Several Italians, particularly in Coalgate, came from that part of the Austrian Tyrol that Italy gained after World War I. During the later stages of immigration, the emphasis gradually changed to southern Italians until the distribution was about equal by 1910. This corresponded roughly with the overall pattern of migration from Italy. Although all parts of southern Italy were represented in Oklahoma, Molise and Sicily provided more immigrants than the other areas. The chief port of departure for southern Italians was Naples, while many of the northern and central Italians left from LaHavre, France. The overwhelming majority of Italians who eventually came to the coalfields of Oklahoma entered the country at New York City.

Italian villages tended to transfer large portions of their population to Oklahoma as in other areas of the United States. In Pittsburg and Latimer counties a number of Sicilians from Calascibetta and Villarosa settled in the coal towns. A small number of immigrants also came from Gubbio in northern Umbria and from the neighboring town of Fabriano across the boundary in the Marches. Several Piedmontese came from Valdieri and Castellamonte. The largest numbers, however, came from a few villages in the Campobasso province in Molise. These hamlets and towns included Agnone, Bagnoli del Trigno, Pietrabbondante, and Castiglione di Carovilli. The second largest group, those from Pietrabbondante, settled in Wilburton. The largest contingent came from Castiglione di Carovilli. Several dozen of these villagers moved to Krebs and later Hartshorne, Wilburton, and other towns to the east. Other immigrants from Carovilli also located in the mining communities of Hubbard, Ohio, and Brookside, Colorado, with many of the residents from Carovilli moving about among those two towns and others in Oklahoma. Illustrating the dominance of that village, about one-half of the Italians who were married in St. Joseph's Catholic Church in Krebs came from Castiglione di Carovilli. In this new and unfamiliar land, the desire to relocate among friends and family from the homeland was understandable.[4]

A good example of the natives of Carovilli as well as an average Italian immigrant was Domenico (Dominic) Rossi. He arrived in Krebs in 1903 when the small town was expanding because of the booming coal industry. Like many Italians who eventually settled in Krebs, Rossi was born in Castiglione di Carovilli on February 16, 1885. Until sixteen years of age, he lived with his family and grew up much like the average peasant farmer in southern Italy. In 1901 an older brother returned from the United States, where he had been a miner in Wyoming, and induced Rossi to return to the New World with him. Tracing the same route that many of their countrymen followed, the two brothers left Carovilli, traveled to Naples, and caught a steamship that took them to New York City. Almost immediately they went to the Denver area and worked in the mines at Lafayette and then further south at Brookside. Rossi left Colorado in 1903 and moved to Krebs.

On April 1, 1903, the day after he arrived, Rossi attended his first major social event in his new home—a large picnic sponsored by the local unit of the United Mine Workers. The first persons who approached him asked if he was going to join the union or if he was going to "scab." Rossi immediately answered that he would become a member, for he favored unions and had been involved in trying to form a local in Colorado. Laborers in the coal fields generally disliked scabs, workers who refused to join the union, and Rossi probably would not have wanted to anger them. Further conforming to the surroundings of his new home, he soon joined the Italian musical band of the Christopher Columbus Mutual Aid Society. In 1909 Rossi married a girl from his home village in Italy, a customary inclination of the Italian immigrants. Eventually they had five children, one of whom died during childhood.

After he had arrived in 1903, Rossi went to work in the mines of the area, laboring most of the time in Krebs at the Osage Coal and Mining Company's mines No. 5 and No. 8. Like other workers in the county, Rossi also sought employment in other communities such as Haileyville and Carbon, but worked in the mines near Krebs more than any other place. In the late 1920s and 1930s, many of the Italian miners moved out of the area to seek employment in other areas such as Akron, Ohio, where at least 200 former residents of Krebs migrated. Rossi stayed in Krebs, however, working in the mines until his retirement in 1948. He died in that town on March 4, 1975, almost seventy-two years after he arrived. He was a typical Italian coal miner, who, at the price of backbreaking labor, experienced a relatively high standard of living in Oklahoma. This was far different from the peasant's life he probably would have lived in southern Italy.

Outside of the four principal counties (Pittsburg, Coal, Latimer, and Okmulgee), lived approximately 340 foreign-born Italians. Of that number, fifty-five lived in other counties where coal mining was also an important part of the economy; therefore, their experience was much the same as in the other mining areas.[5] Eighty-six more resided in towns over 10,000 in population, communities that had diversified job opportunities. Those towns included Oklahoma City, Muskogee, Chickasha, Enid, Guthrie, Shawnee, and Tulsa. The remaining Italians, about 200, lived in rural areas or in communities of less than 10,000 population.[6]

One unique cluster of Italians in Caddo County offers a marked contrast to the patterns in the coal-mining district. After having first settled in the Chicago area, they came to the vicinity of Fort Cobb between 1904 and 1915. In 1910 they numbered fifteen persons born in Italy with eight of their offspring in the county. Ten years later they included twenty-four foreign born, and must have totaled at least forty foreign stock.

The first of the Italians at Fort Cobb was Antonio Caruso. Born near Taormina, Sicily, in 1853, Caruso came to the United States in the 1870s. He moved frequently, even after his marriage in 1884. Eventually he settled in Chicago Heights, a suburb south of Chicago, and worked nearby at the Cuneo Brothers wholesale fruit house. A non-Italian bookkeeper there told Caruso about land in Oklahoma Territory that could be leased at a very cheap rate from Indian owners. After visiting in 1904, he moved with his family to the area of Fort

Cobb. With his *padrone*-like leadership he soon persuaded friends and acquaintances to follow. Eventually settling in the area were several Italian-born immigrants with the surnames of Caruso, Gian Filippo, Nicolosi, Gullos, Ventruella, Palesano, Campagna, and La Corte. Almost all were Sicilian, though the Nicolosis came from northern Italy.

Perhaps those who followed Caruso to the area made their decisions for reasons similar to those of one particular settler, Giovanni Palesano. Living in Chicago Heights with his family, Palesano and his wife grew weary of the urban life and violence that surrounded them. After a man was murdered on the street below his family's apartment, Palesano decided to move. Some old friends, the Campagnas and Ventruellas, had previously invited him to visit their farms at Fort Cobb. Palesano accepted their offer and arrived at Fort Cobb in the middle of an Indian summer in January 1912. Compared to the cold, bleak, and enclosed streets of Chicago Heights, the warm, fertile, and open fields of the Washita River bottom lands were very attractive. After returning home and telling his wife about his visit, he and his family soon traveled to a new home in Oklahoma Territory.

Initially, Palesano, Caruso, and their friends all farmed. This occupation was somewhat unusual in the general American pattern as well as the trend in Oklahoma. An overwhelming majority of Italian immigrants in the United States sought the high-paying jobs and shunned agriculture, which had offered only subsistence living in their homeland. A few settled on truck farms around the urban fringes in the East. Others developed the vineyards in California or lived on farmland in such places as Bryan, Texas, and Tontitown, Arkansas. When the few Italian families moved to the bottom lands surrounding Fort Cobb, they became another minor exception to the Italians' general inclination to avoid farming in the United States.

Initially all the Italians near Fort Cobb leased land from the Indians. Having been farmers or farm laborers in Italy, they soon adjusted to the climate and crops of the Washita valley. Like their non-Italian neighbors they grew cotton, kafir corn, and maize, while also raising a few hogs and cattle. Added to these familiar crops and livestock were the characteristically Italian produce of grapes and garlic grown for home use. Few of these original Italian farmers bought land or became prosperous. Their impact was small even compared to their coal-mining compatriots of eastern Oklahoma; nevertheless the Italians at Fort Cobb were a clear exception to the general trend of settlement in Oklahoma. They were also one of many examples of the forgotten or unnoticed European groups who entered Oklahoma.

Chapter 3

THE ITALIANS AT WORK IN OKLAHOMA

Excluding the few Italians who farmed at Fort Cobb and those who worked at a variety of jobs in the towns of Oklahoma, the immigrants from Italy overwhelmingly came to the state to mine coal. Although it was one of the major economic endeavors in the territory and attracted hundreds of Italians, coal-mining production remained small in the Oklahoma fields compared to that in other areas of the United States. Output continuously constituted only about 1 percent of the nation's total. On the other hand, the Oklahoma coal industry grew at a rate equivalent to the vast expansion of coal mining throughout the United States. Starting with the first small production in 1873, the region reached the commercial level in 1885 with 500,000 tons. By statehood over 3 million tons were being mined annually, and the peak production was over 4.8 million tons in 1920. The tonnage, as well as the proportionate value, declined substantially during the 1920s and 1930s, revived somewhat during World War II, and ceased almost entirely in the 1960s. Generally, the railroads that operated the mines were the chief users of the coal in the early days, but domestic and industrial consumers later became important. The coal, mostly a high-grade bituminous, was sold primarily in Oklahoma and Texas, and in secondary markets in other adjacent states.[1]

More important than the amount of production were the miners who came to the area, for they were instrumental in the settlement of Indian Territory and the subsequent development of Oklahoma. Drawn to the mining fields because of good wages, approximately 1,000 coal miners had entered Indian Territory at the end of the first decade in 1883. Between 1904 and 1920, around 8,000 men were employed in the coal industry. During the most productive years of the coal-mining era, the wages were the highest income anyone could receive in the area, averaging $2.40 per day between 1872 and 1912, and increasing to an average of $6.05 per day between 1913 and 1925. Some mine owners paid by the tonnage, but this system usually approximated the same amount as payments by the day. The Italians and the other early immigrants of the late 1880s found the earnings higher than those in the East. Even as late as 1903, the basic wage of approximately $2.50 per day was higher than in many other areas. The advantages of higher pay were offset by certain local disadvantages. Employment was irregular, and in some years the miners in Oklahoma were fortunate if they worked 200 days. Working conditions were often more dangerous than in other regions.

Coal mining was very tedious everywhere, and Indian Territory was no exception. The working days were long, strenuous, and hazardous. The coal veins in the area usually averaged only four feet in height, and often these narrowed to two feet or less. As a result, the miner stooped or actually worked on his knees much of the time, often in water. If the miner was being paid by the ton, the rocks he dug out of the mine were discarded, and the coal he laboriously extracted was sifted over a screen with only the lump coal being weighed to compute his pay.

With the usual hard labor of the mines came the real danger of mining disasters. As machinery was introduced, as tasks became specialized, and as the mines grew deeper, accidents increased in frequency. However, the old dangers of roof cave-ins, falling coal, and explosions, were part of the potential hazards since the early days. The absence of adequate mining safety laws in Indian Territory increased the number of mishaps. The operators were generally free to follow their natural inclination to emphasize low-cost production over safety, thus increasing the danger and discomfort of the work. Even after Congress passed an act in 1891 that established safety regulations for mines in the territories, the operators were slow to respond. This tardy compliance had tragic consequences. On January 7, 1892, an explosion ripped through Osage Coal and Mining Company's Mine No. 11, immediately killing eighty-seven and injuring about 150 more. Several Italians died or were injured in this mine disaster, the worst in Oklahoma's history. The explosion occurred when a worker routinely fired a shot, but he did so twenty minutes too early while men were leaving the mine at the day's end. Concerning the scene underground, one survivor recalled: "All about me there were agonized groans, shouting, and bedlam. Men were tearing at their flaming clothing, dropping in their tracks."[2] Dozens of local

24

miners helped in the rescue effort with some coming from as far away. as Lehigh. Emergency workers carried the maimed and injured to makeshift hospitals in company houses and private residences.

After this disaster, coal mine owners implemented strict safety rules; nonetheless, numerous accidents occurred in the years that followed. The conditions were so perilous that in 1906 officials reported that one man was killed for every 73,000 tons of coal mined in Indian Territory. This accident rate was much higher than in nearby coal-producing states, and one of the worst in the nation. Following statehood, accidents still occurred frequently despite safety legislation and close inspection. Chief Mine Inspector Pete Hanraty claimed that Oklahoma had the most dangerous mines in the United States. Italians were involved in many of the mine disasters, and in a single year, July 1, 1909, to June 30, 1910, seventeen of them died in fifty-one fatal accidents in Oklahoma.

Workers originally were classified as simply either skilled "miners" or inexperienced "helpers." In the 1870s and 1880s, almost all of the skilled miners were either British or Americans, but the unskilled helpers came from other ethnic groups. The Italians, when they arrived, were particularly ignorant of proper mining techniques and had a reputation of being reckless miners. After four years of experience, however, the novices were considered skilled. By 1900 mechanization and specialization brought about several new classifications: weighmen, tophands, master mechanics, hoisting engineers, slope engineers, firemen, and others. Many Italians worked in almost every capacity in the mines though miners of English-speaking nationalities remained in the supervisory positions. Few Italians took the Oklahoma State Mining Board's examinations, which were required for engineers, fire bosses, pit bosses, and superintendents. The board, formed in 1908, sought to give tests for those four important positions in order to improve the safety and efficiency of the mines. Of the 969 tests first given between 1908 and 1911, approximately twenty-four Italians took the examinations, only about 2.5 percent of the total. Although this percentage increased in the 1920s, the proportionate number of Italians taking and passing the tests remained quite small.

Regardless of what positions the Italians held, coal mining was the most important economic factor in their new lives in Oklahoma. An overwhelming majority of Italians who came to the state worked as miners until the decline of the mines in the 1920s. Thus for years coal mining greatly affected the lives of the Italians. It brought the Italians together with other nationalities in the mines. It offered wages

Mine No. 15 at Alderson. Several of the miners in the picture are Italian. Courtesy of Mrs. Anna Maffioli.

sufficient to allow mobility. And it forced them to find other livelihoods during the years of its decline.

Labor unions substantially affected the conditions in the mines, and helped to form closer relations between the Italians and their fellow workers. The relative peacefulness, collective bargaining, and general nature of the labor unions in Oklahoma little resembled the radical labor organizations of Italy, indicating that any violent tendencies were moderated by conditions in their new home. In Italy, both agricultural and industrial workers formed unions in response to their poverty and social immobility. In 1864 a law made all labor unions virtually illegal, a situation unchanged until 1889. Workers joined mutual-aid societies and other cooperative organizations as early as 1860. These groups gradually developed into trade unions, first among the industrial workers in the 1870s and then among the agricultural laborers in the 1880s. In 1906 these unions combined into the General Confederation of Labor.

One of the most useful tools of the labor unions was the strike, and with more frequent strikes came increasing violence. Over 600 strikes occurred in Italy between 1870 and 1878, but after attitudes and laws became more lenient, the number increased even more. Italian immigrants in the United States, including Oklahoma, joined labor organizations that were much less violent and showed little resemblance to the unions in the homeland. In general, Italian participation in the unions throughout the nation was similar to Italian involvement in Oklahoma. Initially, Americans and British immigrants in the labor unions excluded the Italians, as well as other southern and eastern Europeans, from membership. The Italians, in many cases, entered the labor market as unwitting strikebreakers. At other times, they worked knowingly for lower wages than their Anglo-Saxon counterparts. Many early and some later Italian immigrants simply refused to take interest in labor organizations because they considered America as only a temporary residence. They wanted to make good wages, save some money, and return home. Gradually, however, the old barriers deteriorated as many Italians decided to make America their home. Also many labor leaders realized the advantages of bringing the immigrant workers into the union fold.

The unusual legal situation in Indian Territory posed a problem that labor unions did not encounter elsewhere. Among the Indian Nations of present-day eastern Oklahoma, the miners were guests, subject to removal at the whims of the Indian leaders. In other areas of the United States, mine operators sometimes ousted miners from the coal fields, often with military or police aid. This was a questionable practice if not extralegal. In Indian Territory, however, there was no doubt. The federal government was bound by treaties to remove the miners forcibly when the tribes demanded it. This power constantly threatened the success of any strikes. The Indians, as owners of royalty, opposed strikes and expediently sided with the railroads and other mine owners, who ironically were a major force in pressuring for the dissolution of tribal government.

The Noble Order of the Knights of Labor, the first important American labor union to affect the area, was organized nationally in 1879, and came to the coal fields of Indian Territory in 1883. Initially the organization made no effort to attract southern and eastern Europeans to join because they accepted lower wages than Americans and British immigrants. However, some Italians participated in the strike of 1894, which the Knights of Labor called to protest a 25 percent reduction in wages. The Choctaws, losing money from the strike, persuaded the Commissioner of Indian Affairs to send troops to expel the striking miners. Approximately 350 troublesome miners were forced from their homes at gunpoint and shipped to Arkansas by rail. Italians were among them, and the Italian government protested their expulsion to the United States Department of State. Many of the miners who were deported immediately returned

27

to their homes in Indian Territory, but with a 20 percent reduction in their wages. Shortly thereafter, the Knights of Labor ceased to exist in both Indian Territory and the nation as a whole. Widespread internal dissension and unfavorable public opinion against that union forced laborers to turn elsewhere for their leadership.[3]

Soon the more efficient and better organized United Mine Workers of America replaced the Knights of Labor in the mining fields. Founded nationally in 1890, the first local in Indian Territory was established at Krebs in 1898. As with the Knights of Labor, the English-speaking miners led the new union and directed most of the labor disputes. The Italians showed much more interest in the organization than the other southern and eastern Europeans, and many held minor offices or were on pit committees, which helped settle disputes at the mines. However, the general attitude of most Italians was indifference; they joined because it was necessary. Often a new miner in the area would be approached upon arriving and sternly asked if he was going to join the union. Under such pressure to conform, the Italians generally chose membership. Many communities in the coal fields had locals which included Italians. For instance, in 1909, 87 percent of the dues-paying members of Local No. 2327 in Krebs were Italians.

In trying to gain concessions from the operators, the miners utilized collective bargaining through union representatives. Union officials, armed with provisions of contracts that had been signed by the operators, traveled extensively, representing the miners in many disputes. Sometimes the officials settled arguments between members within the various locals. For instance, one local called upon its representative to settle a dispute between the miners who wanted to be paid by the ton and those who wanted to be paid a daily wage. The most frequent duties of the union officials, however, included the investigation of poor working conditions and unfair dismissal of employees. Complaints about these matters ranged from humorous annoyances to serious grievances. For example, one miner, who belonged to Local No. 2327 in Krebs and worked at Osage Mine No. 5, protested against what he believed was an intolerable situation. He refused to drive a certain mule that was so "notorious for her stinking qualities anyone who drives her are [sic] unable to eat dinner."[4] Because of his refusal to work with the animal, the miner was laid off for two days until the mule was replaced. After an exchange of letters between the union local and the district office, the unfortunate worker learned that nothing in the union contract covered stinking mules or any similar undesirable aspects of work.

Although some episodes were somewhat frivolous, most involved much more weighty matters. One Italian miner, for instance, wrote union officials: "Please come to McAlester as soon as you can because the boss of No. 1 in Carbon Oklahoma fired me out the mine and I like to see you about it. [sic] I think I have been treated wrongly."[5] The necessity of action on such complaints revealed the importance of the union.

The United Mine Workers also used the strike as a weapon in their efforts to improve the working conditions of the laborers. The prolonged strike that occurred between 1898 and 1903 brought several benefits for the miners, as did some of the subsequent strikes in 1910, 1916, 1919, and 1920. There was little real violence during these strikes, particularly among the Italians. Even the coal operators agreed that the Italians and other southern and eastern Europeans were less extravagant and insistent in their demands. If any radical action appeared in the mining area, it was usually instigated by the immigrants from the British Isles and Americans rather than the natives of Italy. Thus the violence that characterized the labor disputes of Italy was not found in the union movement of Oklahoma. The miners generally engaged in collective bargaining and relatively peaceful strikes to gain benefits from the operators.

John Marino, Sr., of the second generation, became a local leader in the United Mine Workers in Pittsburg County. His inclination to work peacefully within the system differed from the violent attitude of the labor leaders in Italy. The son of Gregorio and Katrina Marino, he was born on September 10, 1891, in Hartshorne, Oklahoma. His father, originally from Salerno, had migrated to the area in 1885 and worked in the coal mines for most of his working life. Experiencing firsthand the hazards and unacceptable consequences of inaction, the elder Marino became one of the first Italians to realize the importance of organizing the workers. On January 7, 1892, he narrowly escaped the explosion that killed 100 people in the Osage Coal and Mining Company Mine No. 11 at Krebs. Later, he helped organize the strike in 1894 and was shipped out of Indian Territory with other strike leaders when Choctaw leaders sided with the mine operators. He taught his son John the importance of working within the union and a general appreciation of hard work. As a boy, he tended the family garden and worked at numerous chores on the small family farm. Marino also attended the Catholic school in Krebs until he was fourteen. At that age he quit school and joined his father in the mines. Between 1905 and 1930 he worked primarily in the coal industry in Pittsburg County. He also found employment in the Goodyear Company in Akron, Ohio, and served in the army in France during World War I.

After the war, he returned to Krebs and resumed his life as a coal miner. Remembering his father's advice never to "scab" and always support the union, Marino became recording secretary for Local No. 2327 in Krebs, a position he held throughout the 1920s. He respected the successful system of arbitration that had developed between the union and the operators.

In his experience with the union, the local won almost every dispute that arose between the miners and the management. The proper method of voicing a complaint followed a well-defined procedure during Marino's terms as secretary. The miner would tell the president or some other officer of the union about his grievance; in turn, the problem was referred to the special three-man pit committee that handled such affairs. They would take the complaint to the pit boss who represented the operator in the discussion. If the pit boss would not comply with the request of the pit committee, they went to the superintendent who managed the mines. While the committee talked to the superintendent, no miners would go to work until the question was settled in favor of the miner who had made the complaint. The representatives of the union board for the region often had become involved in the procedure by this time. Probably because the miners almost always won the arguments under this system, leaders like Marino had little cause to resort to radical methods. He continued to work as a coal miner and as secretary of the union until 1930 when he became a barber, an occupation he learned in the army during World War I.

Like the labor unions, the Socialist party of Oklahoma was another organization closely associated with coal mining. Many Italians in Oklahoma joined the party or at least sympathized with it. Outside of the coalfields the Oklahoma party attracted numerous tenant farmers in the southern portions of the state with a watered-down socialism that seemed like populism in disguise. The doctrines in the coalfields were more recognizable to the ideologically pure believers, but socialists in the Oklahoma coalfields, including the Italians, were far less radical than their European counterparts.[6]

After statehood, Socialists from the national party concentrated enormous effort in Oklahoma, and some of their most able and clever organizers gained large followings. Because of their efforts, the party became one of the strongest in the nation. In 1910 the Socialist party of Oklahoma had 5,842 paid-up members, more than any other state. The state subsequently recorded a higher percentage of Socialist votes than any state, with 16.4 percent in 1912, 21 percent in 1914, and 15.6 percent in 1916.[7]

The strongest element of the party was composed of tenant farmers throughout the southern half of Oklahoma. Most of these members had turned to socialism after the Populist party failed to meet its goals. The farmers' influence distorted the party into an agency that crusaded primarily for agricultural reform in the old Populist tradition. The Socialist party in Oklahoma was far more concerned with the local economic and political issues of the state than with philosophical arguments or distant conflicts between proletariat and bourgeoisie. Nevertheless, the Socialists of Oklahoma did not totally ignore the basic goals of socialism. Particularly in the coalfields it preached for the seizure of the powers of the government to aid workers and to form a classless society. These ideas appealed to the Italians and other miners in eastern Oklahoma. One section of the party platform of 1912 demanded that orgainzed miners, rather than the general public or governor, choose mine inspectors. The platform also called for state ownership of certain industries, including the coal mines. Finally, its provisions for the unemployed and its condemnation of the use of police power in strikes must have been attractive to the miners.

Socialist ideas were not new to the miners, who had been acquainted with these doctrines in other mining regions. Several of the labor leaders became Socialist candidates and received substantial support from the mining regions. The party had strong organization in the coal-mining counties, with committeemen representing most of the precincts. In 1914, 26 percent of the votes were cast for the Socialist gubernatorial candidate in Pittsburg County. In nearby Coal County, candidates of the Socialist party consistently placed second in the electoral contests of 1914.

The precise extent of Italian involvement in the Socialist party was unclear. In 1911 the Senate's special Immigration Commission reported that radical political leaders controlled Italians in certain areas of Oklahoma. According to voting statistics, a substantial number of Italians in some communities, such as Krebs, seemed to be involved in the party. At least they voted for Socialists in the elections.

31

In 1914, the Socialist senatorial candidate, Patrick Nagle, received ninety-three votes in Krebs, just seven votes less than the Democratic front-runner, Thomas Gore, and well ahead of the Republican candidate. The proportion of votes for other offices was similar; indeed, the Socialist party was the second strongest in Krebs during that election year. Most Italians were not citizens, but Italians clearly cast a portion of these votes in Krebs, since they made up more than one-half of the population of that city. The Italians involved with the Socialist party as with the labor union, were usually led by the Anglo-Saxon element. There was also little violence in the history of the Socialist party in Oklahoma. The only important example of violent action was the farmers' revolt of 1917, known as the "Green Corn Rebellion." This disturbance was a response to America's involvement in World War I, and no foreign element participated in the insurrection. Unlike its Italian counterpart, the Socialist party of Oklahoma avoided extralegal coercion and chose instead electoral and legal alternatives.

The career and activities of a prominent Italian Socialist leader, Emilio C. Marianelli, further illustrated this temperate and moderate attitude. He was born in Iron Mountain, Michigan, in 1888, the son of Nazzareno and Margherita Marianelli from Sigillo near Perugia. Although American born, he lived in Italy as a child and received some of his education there. After returning to the United States while still a boy, he worked as a miner at night and, during the day, attended Wyoming Seminary at Kingston, Pennsylvania. He was well acquainted with the hardships of a miner's life.

After graduating from Wyoming Seminary, Marianelli enrolled in the Dickinson School of Law in Carlisle, Pennsylvania. There he developed a friendship with Albert Exendine, a Delaware Indian from Oklahoma who had been an All-American end at the famed Carlisle Indian School. The two friends graduated from law school in 1912 and established a joint practice in Anadarko, Oklahoma, where Exendine's influence was expected to attract clients. The practice proved to be less than satisfactory, however, and the young lawyers began looking for a new and more advantageous area. Hearing that substantial numbers of Italians lived near Krebs, Marianelli visited the area, found it promising, and persuaded his friend to open their new office in nearby McAlester. Although they chose McAlester to open their new practice, many of the clients lived in Krebs and other Italian communities. Whereas Exendine had not been able to attract a sufficient quantity of Indian patrons, Marianelli succeeded in drawing a number of Italian clients.

Until his departure from McAlester in 1927, Marianelli was affiliated with the Socialist party. Immediately before World War I, he and Exendine helped prominent socialist advocate Oscar Ameringer to establish a statewide socialist newspaper, *The Oklahoma Leader*. Marianelli had planned to run for attorney general on the Socialist ticket in 1918, but was drafted to serve in World War I. His description of army life showed him to be far from the stereotype of the socialist radical. Rather than denouncing the war as a product of capitalist imperialism or advocating the use of wartime confusion to advance the socialist program, Marianelli reported that he was actually enjoying army life and making a success of it. He had been promoted to the rank of sergeant and dealt with military insurance matters for soldiers in France. After returning home, Marianelli became a charter member of the American Legion in McAlester—an organization hardly sympathetic to radicalism—and a deacon in the First Baptist Church of McAlester. He remained active in both of these organizations for the rest of his life, further confounding the socialist stereotype. After unsuccessful bids for the position of justice of the state supreme court on the Socialist party ticket, Marianelli moved to Pennsylvania in 1927 where he carried on a vigorous law practice until his death in 1972.

Southern Baptist and Legionnaire, Marianelli was a typical Oklahoma socialist. Like others in the mining region, he became interested in the Socialist party because it promised reforms in the mining industry. His position as chief counsel for the United Mine Workers of Oklahoma in the 1920s and his subsequent assumption of a similar post in Wilkes-Barre, Pennsylvania, indicated that he was concerned and dedicated to the miners' cause. He was a socialist, but not a "radical."

Whether or not most of the Italians joined the Socialist party, almost all worked in the coal mines and belonged to the union, at least when they first arrived. Many of the Italians, as well as other immigrants, also worked at additional part-time jobs or took boarders into their homes to bolster their incomes. Gradually some Italians left the mines to establish businesses or to work at employment less dangerous and less tedious than mining. Few Italians were professionals. The attorney Emilio Marianelli served the Italians and other miners. Dr. Umberto Buffo, an Italian physician, practiced medicine

Luigi Messina's bakery in Haileyville, about 1912. Courtesy of Albert Messina.

in McAlester between 1904 and 1910. He offered an early-day health plan that allowed miners to pay their bills on a monthly basis. Most Italians, however, were generally unskilled or had nonprofessional trades that they had learned in the homeland.

Some Italians also owned and operated various businesses. In 1905, Adolfo Rossi, the emigration official from Italy who visited Oklahoma, reported that Italians operated seven or eight general merchandise or grocery stores in Krebs. Six years later the Senate's Immigration Commission, which investigated conditions nationwide, noted that many Italians owned small grocery stores, bakeries, restaurants, or other businesses throughout the coal-mining region. According to the commission's report, several Italians controlled stock in a large mercantile store in Coalgate. Also in that town, a few Italians owned stock in a large grocery and dry goods store which was originally created solely for Italian customers. In both Coalgate and Hartshorne some Italians owned partial interest in a local bank.

Business directories for the state during 1912, 1913, and 1916 confirmed the findings of Rossi and the Immigration Commission. According to those directories, Italians owned more local grocery or

Grocery and general merchandise store owned by Giovanni Battista Carletti, Haileyville, about 1910. Courtesy of Mrs. Tony Ravaoili.

general merchandise stores than any other businesses. Next in frequency were meat markets and bakeries. Other Italians were barbers, poolroom owners, carpenters, blacksmiths, stonecutters, peddlers, and restaurant operators. In 1916 one Italian, Dominic Antonelli, was listed as "Manager of the Italian Department" in a McAlester bank.

The life stories and occupations of many of the non-mining Italians were reflected in the biographies of three particular men: Giusseppe (Joseph) Fassino, a grocer and owner of a macaroni factory; Pietro Piegari (Pete Prichard), a restaurateur; and Carmine (Carl) Finamore, a butcher and rancher. The first of these Italians to settle in the area was Joseph Fassino. Born in the small village of Canischio on September 9, 1863, he was a member of a poor farming family, the son of Carlo and Angela Fassino. As a boy, he helped with the family chores and duties, and at age ten quit school and went to work as a shepherd. Later, like many Italians in the northern part of the country, he migrated to Switzerland and France to work on various construction projects, including the St. Gotthard Tunnel in the Alps. He returned to Italy when he was drafted in 1883. After three years he was discharged and decided to leave Italy. Fassino particularly hated the economic hardships and virtual lack of opportunities, vowing not to raise a family if he had to remain in Italy. He left for the United States in 1886, age twenty-three.

After arriving at New York City, Fassino immediately joined an older brother in Braidwood, Illinois, where he worked in the coal mines. He also lived in other neighboring coal-mining communities, including Norris, Illinois, the new town of many people from his old village. In 1887, John Fassino, a younger brother, joined the family members already in Illinois. After a short period of time the oldest brother returned to Italy. Joe and John Fassino, having tried farming, decided to use their savings and go into business. They heard that several Italians lived in Indian Territory and that no one had opened a grocery store there for the Italian population. In 1891 the two Fassino brothers moved to Krebs and opened a small store that sold foods that their countrymen wanted. The Fassinos prospered and became leaders of the colony.

As a grocer and businessman, Joe Fassino took uncommon measures to meet the needs of his fellow countrymen. On several occasions he smuggled his food into a nearby company camp for sale to Italian families who desired special items such as cheese, figs, and chestnuts. These Italian miners were not allowed to buy products except from the company store, which had few of the particular goods they wanted. The camps were fenced and guarded, but Fassino, implying that he wanted to visit friends, hid the food in his buggy and took it to customers who wanted the imported items. During strikes, the Fassino brothers extended credit to the miners, often almost causing bankruptcy for themselves. Because of this, many people in the area continued to buy from their store. They also allowed many Italians in the area to use their store as a bank, and Joe Fassino kept accounts of all savings and records of wills in case the depositors died. These activities expanded as he began handling certain business affairs and correspondence for patrons. Because of these services, he became the Italian consular agent around the turn of the century and kept the position for a number of years, issuing passports, exchanging currency, and performing other services for Italian immigrants.

Despite the loss of their deposits because of a bank closure, in 1897 the Fassino brothers decided to expand their enterprises by opening a macaroni factory in McAlester. Taking a risk, they soon regained their previous prosperity and continued with their plans to establish the factory. In May of 1897, they received word that the machinery was on its way to McAlester, a bit of news that soon became common knowledge. The *South McAlester Capital* reported the story, pointing out the fine character of the Fassino Brothers: "They are two energetic men who have gone into the business with their own capital and who will add to the city an industry that will bring them and the city deserved reputation."[8]

By October 1897, sales from the factory were sufficient to encourage Joe Fassino to search for outlets in Kansas, where he found a ready market. Eventually the market area included Oklahoma, Kansas, Texas, Missouri, Arkansas, and a surplus sales region in the Caribbean. By 1902 the successful Fassino brothers again expanded their business enterprises when they began selling wagons and buggies. Also in that year they moved their residence from Krebs to

Joe Fassino and family in their 1912 Moon automobile. Clearly apparent is the high degree of affluence Fassino achieved as owner of the McAlester Macaroni Factory. Courtesy of Mrs. Charles Fassino.

McAlester where they soon became recognized leaders in the community. One early description of the Italians in the area explained: "The richest and most intelligent Italians located here are said to be the Fassino Brothers, the Piedmontese proprietors of a macaroni factory and of a carriage and wagon warehouse."[9] By 1905 the Fassinos had invested at least $60,000 in land in the area, which they considered a safe and profitable investment.

The two brothers continued to help develop the area during the remainder of their lives. Leaving the businesses for his brother to run, Joe Fassino retired in 1928. He died on August 2, 1936. He and his brother had been the first Italians to gain a position of prominence in Pittsburg County. Together they built one of the area's largest manufacturing companies, demonstrating a talent and adeptness in American business procedures. Joe Fassino became a leader among the Italians, being called the "dean" of the Italians in the region at the time of his death.

Another Italian who came over as a child and who learned a new livelihood out of necessity was Pete Prichard. He was born Pietro Piegari on June 29, 1895, at San Gregario Magne, Italy. He changed his name to Prichard when he began working in the coalfields of Oklahoma. Prichard's father first came to the area about 1902 and a year later sent for his wife and children, including Pete. Having received less than three years of education, Prichard began working in the mines at eleven years of age. He also spent several months in Arkansas working with a railroad, then returned to the mines where he was injured in 1916 at twenty-one years of age. His leg was crushed so badly that he could not return to mining. He then worked at any available job and began making and selling "Choc" (Choctaw) beer, a local homemade brew, in his home in Krebs.

His customers often brought bread, sausages, and cheese with them when they gathered to drink beer in his home. Realizing the possibility of a steady source of income, Prichard started providing foods for his patrons. Soon the small enterprise became a thriving restaurant. As a child, Prichard had enjoyed cooking, often stealing out of the house with his mother's frying pan to cook the quarry that he and some young fellow hunters had killed. Also, while working in the railroad in Arkansas, some Greek immigrants instructed him on the art of preparing food. Using this early-acquired interest and experience in cooking, Prichard formally began his restaurant at his home in 1925. With many of the ingredients homemade, he served spaghetti, meatballs, ravioli, sausage, and other Italian dishes, along with salad, chicken, steak, and other conventional foods. Unfortunately he continued selling his own domestic "Choc" beer, for which he was arrested in 1932. Thereafter he discontinued offering the illicit liquid refreshment and operated a completely legitimate restaurant at his home.

During the Depression "Pete's Place" thrived as the reputation of his excellent Italian dishes spread throughout the region. In 1932 he made an addition to his cafe by building an extra room, and again expanded by boxing in his back porch in 1938. Other enlargements followed in similar fashion until he had completely converted his home into an eating establishment. Throughout his years of operation, Prichard drew as customers every governor of the state since the 1930s, as well as actors, consuls, ambassadors, and other prominent persons. He sold Pete's Place to his son Bill in 1961 and retired completely in 1966. Prichard died on May 1, 1970, in Krebs. An example of those Italians who were forced to find work outside of the mines, Prichard chose to make a hobby into an occupation and succeeded.

Another Italian who used skills he had learned as a child was Carmine Finamore. A native of Bagnoli del Trigno, Finamore was born on October 23, 1889. As a boy he worked as a shepherd near his home. Also he learned the techniques of butchering, for his father, Domenico Finamore, and grandfather were butchers in the village. Young Finamore not only mastered the basic skills of slaughtering, skinning, and dressing sheep and goats, he also observed first-hand the talents and tricks of bargaining with farmers for their animals.

During his early twenties, young Finamore left his family's shop and the village and traveled to Rome. There he worked in a stable and station house for horse-drawn cabs. At the end of each day he cleaned and washed down the carriages and tended to the horses. Each morning he harnessed the animals and prepared the vehicles for use. After four years of work at about four *lire* per day, Finamore saved enough to emigrate to America. He returned to his village, told his parents he wanted to leave, and soon departed for America with four friends from his home village. The young men traveled to Naples by train where they embarked on the *Duca D' Aosta* for New York. After arriving at Ellis Island, on October 18, 1916, Finamore, and possibly the other members of the group, traveled to Fairmont, West Virginia, where other friends from Bagnoli del Trigno worked in a paper mill. Young Finamore worked there for several months at two dollars a day. Meanwhile an older sister, living in Krebs, sent letter after letter asking him to join her at her community. He eventually surrendered to her persistent requests and moved to Krebs to work in the mines.

In 1918 Finamore married Maria Narducci, who had been born in Italy but had lived in Krebs since infancy. Sometime later he decided to quit mining because of a near-fatal accident. He was setting wooden props to support the ceiling in the mine when a massive slab of rock slammed to the floor inches from him. Except for luck, Finamore would have been crushed. He was scared. The next day he told his boss at the mine that he was not going to work again. His boss wanted to know why. Finamore answered him: "Well, work yourself down the mine. I no wanna' come down there. You think I'm goin' go die down there?"[10] Finamore, like many other miners who experienced similar accidents, never returned to the mines.

Afterwards, he began relying on his old trade—butchering. An Italian friend in Krebs suggested that Finamore buy a small wagon and begin selling fresh meat to the miners in town. Finamore soon learned that a lady who lived east of Krebs owned several hundred goats. He visited the woman, bought five or six goats at a time, butchered them, loaded the dressed meat in an icebox in the wagon, and peddled the meat at the miners' houses. Finamore gradually expanded his operations and included beef and other types of meat in his business. Unfortunately his trade was dependent largely on the coal miners. When their industry began declining, so did Finamore's income.

Along with many of his countrymen Finamore left the economically depressed coalfields of Oklahoma for employment in Ohio. At Youngstown in 1927 he worked in a rubber factory and was a butcher for a local market in his spare time. Eventually his frugality paid off. The new money he made, added to his substantial savings from Oklahoma, totaled over $2,000—not a small sum in the late 1920s. With these savings Finamore dreamed of buying his own land. In 1929 Finamore, through his brother-in-law in Krebs, bought 320 acres of land in default at a bank auction. Quickly gathering his family and belongings, he returned to Oklahoma, claimed his land east of Krebs, and resumed his life as a butcher with his own land for his own cattle. Finamore supplied several grocers and a cafe with meat while also selling his products through the icehouse in McAlester that refrigerated and stored his beef. For years many of Finamore's customers considered his products the best in the area. Now in retirement, he lives in Krebs and continues to raise a few cattle on his land.

Finamore the butcher, like Prichard the restaurateur and Fassino the grocer and businessman, left the mines for a new livelihood. The descriptions of their lives resembled the patterns of many non-mining Italians in the area. They were miners upon arriving, and then because of fear, injury, or good sense, they left coal mining. They undertook new enterprises that, in many cases, they had learned as boys in their homeland or in America. Yet they also adapted to the requirements and demands of business in their new homes. Most were frugal and industrious, many were successful and prosperous.

Chapter 4

ITALIAN CUSTOMS AND
SOCIAL INSTITUTIONS IN OKLAHOMA

Whether the Italians who immigrated to Oklahoma came from the cool, alpine north, or the dry, rocky central Apennines, or the arid Mediterranean coastal plains of Italy, they found a terrain and climate in Oklahoma that was much different. Unlike the usual stereotype of Oklahoma, much of the eastern section of the state, including the coal-mining region, is mountainous or hilly. Coal County is relatively flat with rolling terrain; however, in the remaining areas the low hills and mountains predominate with small blackjack and post oak trees. Between the hills are both narrow and broad valleys that are open prairies in some areas and wooded bottom lands in other places. In the eastern section of the region pine trees appear while the hills become more mountainlike. Throughout the coalfields the climate is temperate with substantial rainfall in the spring and distinct seasonal variations of temperature.

Regardless of the differences in weather or terrain, living conditions in the coal-mining communities of Oklahoma were not a totally pleasing experience, particularly during the days of Indian Territory. When the first Italians drifted to the area, few houses were available in this generally unsettled country of the Choctaw Indians. As a result, the miners almost totally depended on the "company." They were forced to live in company houses, and were paid in scrip good only at the company store. The houses usually were one-story, one-family dwellings, containing from three to five rooms. Poorly built with cheap lumber, these homes were in constant need of repair and were little more than shacks.

The situation gradually improved, however, as permanent settlements grew up around the mines. The workers were given an option of living either in company houses or in homes of their own choosing.

At the same time, conditions in many of the company houses were ameliorated. Also, drawing scrip for pay became voluntary and was used only when a miner was short of funds between pay checks. Italians were frugal and seldom drew scrip for pay.

Even with the restrictions of the old company system, the living conditions of the miners were tolerable and, in most instances, an improvement over those in Italy. Water systems and other conveniences eventually were added. Many Italians also began buying their own town lots and homes, although landownership was restricted to townsites as the Indians held the rest of the land in common until statehood. The frugality of the Italians and good wages of the coal mines also enabled the Italians to save enough money to send back home or to return with it. Whereas opportunities had been limited in Italy, they abounded in Indian Territory, and the Italians gained a real economic mobility that had been impossible in Italy.

The quality and variety of their food offered the most vivid contrast between living conditions in the old country and in Oklahoma. In Italy the peasant's diet was meager, consisting of dark bread, minestrone, mush, wine, and very little meat. In Oklahoma, small bakeries provided an ample amount of white bread, and meat was included in almost every meal. Some Italians cultivated vegetable gardens. Thus the Italians of Oklahoma were able to fulfill the simple necessity for nourishment. The meeting of this basic need, along with the newly attained mobility, improved the quality of life and eventually promoted assimilation and change.

Probably one of the most important changes that took place in the Italians' lives was the inevitable transformation and Americanization of the family unit. In Italy the peasant family was patriarchal—a well-defined unit with the father as head and with every member having a strong sense of responsibility for the other members of the family. The father not only assigned the chores and responsibilities to the children but also provided the family with necessities. He was seldom disputed in a decision concerning the family. The eldest son and mother advised the father, however, and had at least some power in the decision-making process.

In Italy the woman acknowledged her husband as family head; yet she carried out certain duties that were no less important. The mother took charge of rearing the children, insuring their religious instruction, and preparing them for marriage. She also articulated the social relations of the family. The children were particularly obedient largely because of the severe punishment that they received when they chose to defy their parents. They were taught to have a strong regard for the family, and they usually considered the effect on the whole family before making a personal decision.

A vast majority of the Italians who came to the United States settled in large cities such as New York where the traditions of the family were greatly altered. The father, working in a factory, had less contact with and less control over the family. The Italian mother often worked in a garment shop and lost much authority over the children, though she also gained a new sense of autonomy because of her new contacts outside the family. Further altering the family structure in the American cities was the new independence of the children who became more rebellious as they made acquaintances with a large number of children in their neighborhoods. If the family unit deteriorated, it was largely because of the distance between the parents and children.

In Oklahoma the situation differed substantially. The coal-mining area did not present the same problems as the urban areas. The patriarchal family unit remained an accepted way of life to most of the immigrants as well as Americans in the rural and small-town atmosphere. Few of the conflicts with tradition existed in Oklahoma as they did in the eastern cities where the family unit easily deteriorated. The father of the Italian family in Oklahoma retained much of his authority. During territorial days the children had little opportunity to go to school, and some parents, particularly southern Italians, sometimes deliberately kept the children from going to school. Many parents also insisted that the children speak only Italian at home; as a result, many children had little chance to learn English and assimilation was slow in the early days.

If any member of the Italian family in Oklahoma was slow to change, it was the immigrant woman. Because the Italians lived in colonies, the women had little cause to associate with people other than those of their own nationalistic background. Unlike the large cities in other parts of the country, there were no factories where Italian women could work and find a certain degree of independence from their husbands. Even domestic service was not available in the area, for only a small number of people could afford maids or household servants. If their husbands owned businesses, the Italian wives sometimes worked as clerks or assistants, but this was not frequent. Otherwise, the only consequential economic activity, involving about one-fourth of the Italian women in Oklahoma, was the providing of rooms and service for boarders. Since mostly Italian men took the rooms, renting did not bring many Italian women into contact with those outside their nationality.[1]

The immigrant Italian women in Oklahoma, virtually isolated from contact with the larger community, had lives that were centered on the home. Very few Italian women over twenty years of age were unmarried, and the daily routine and tasks were much like those undertaken by American women in other rural areas or small towns in the late nineteenth and early twentieth centuries. Clothes were washed by hand or on a rubboard, and cheese and sausage were made at home for the family. Most Italian women baked their own bread. Almost every backyard had a stone or brick oven that the wife heated once or twice a week to cook twenty to thirty loaves. Sometimes neighbors would undertake these household tasks jointly, particularly if a wife was ill or giving birth. Partially because of tradition and because of the slow transportation and lack of medical facilities, almost all Italian women gave birth to their children at home often attended only by midwives. Yet all was not hardship for Italian women. Sometimes when the men were at work, or more often on Sunday, the wives would meet, converse, cook, and crochet or embroider.

Rose Duca, a popular and well-known Italian from Hartshorne. "Grandma Duca," as she was generally known, was one of the first Italian women in Indian Territory, arriving in 1887. Courtesy of Albert Messina.

Most of the interactions among the Italian women were within their own group. Because only about one-fourth of the Italian women in the area could speak English and because most homes were conveniently located in an Italian colony, the Italian immigrant women relied on few things that were not Italian. There was even an Italian grocer in most neighborhoods who provided the necessary foodstuffs, often delivering items to each home. As a result, many Italian immigrant women of the area lived most of their lives in small communities, traded with Italian merchants, and never learned to speak English.

Although certain forces worked against the assimilation and Americanization of first-generation Italian women, their husbands and children came into contact with other forces that caused them to change. The coal mines and labor unions brought the men into contact with men of other nationalities and with methods that were characteristically American. Those Italian men who worked outside of the mines often came into contact with American businessmen and were particularly changed because of it. With the coming of statehood and compulsory education, the children of the Italian immigrants were thrust into schools where they inevitably changed due to contact with American children and the English language.

One part of the Italian culture that predominated was the tradition of courtship and marriage. A few of the southern Italians continued to arrange marriages for their children as they had done in Italy, but this was not widespread. In many instances Italian bachelors wrote relatives back home who selected a young woman and arranged a marriage. Often the bride and groom had never met; sometimes the girl had been a childhood sweetheart.

For those young Italians who met, courted, and married in Oklahoma, the customs and traditions of the old country were steadfastly observed. Fathers of Italian girls often thwarted the designs of love-stricken young men. Only the most respectable male suitors dared to call on young women. Courtship was not a frivolous pastime, but was a prelude to marriage.

Once a young woman's family gave permission for courtship, strict rules were followed. Almost all contact between the unmarried man and woman was in the home of the woman's parents. The couple was never alone since one or more relatives attended the pair as they conversed and interacted. Maria Finamore, a resident of Krebs, recalled vividly this element of courtship: "For a while he sat in one corner and I sat at the other corner and an uncle was in be-

An Italian wedding in North McAlester in 1925. The groom is Battista Maffeo and the bride is Onorina Francisco. Courtesy of Mrs. Minnie Cioni.

tween us."[2] Later in the courtship the couple was allowed to take walks—with a chaperon. The unmarried young man and woman could venture into public unattended only when they visited relatives and friends to announce their engagement and to extend invitations to the wedding.

Italian weddings in Oklahoma were usually large and joyous affairs. Most were held in the home of the parents of the bride or groom, and every relative of the extended family attended if possible. After a simple ceremony a celebration followed with plenty of food, drinks, and sometimes dancing. This type of wedding and the old rules for courtship lasted well into the 1930s. In later years, however, subsequent generations faced fewer restrictions on their courtships and more Americanized weddings.

Many of the changes in courtship and marriage as well as other customs were the result of the new atmosphere of the communities in Oklahoma. Whether the town was strictly a company town or was open to everyone, the typical community in Oklahoma seemed very different from the isolated villages that earlier had been the homes for many of the Italian immigrants. Although the Italians in Oklahoma segregated themselves more than any other immigrant group, it was impossible to escape the somewhat cosmopolitan atmosphere of the coal-mining communities. Nevertheless, some of their culture and lifestyle was preserved because they banded together in colonies.

The Italian communities provided social interaction and events that not only enhanced the quality of life in the coal-mining towns but also preserved some of the customs of the old country. The socially-minded visited other homes, often drinking homemade "Choc" beer and eating sausage or other foods. Traveling troupes of singers frequently visited McAlester, Krebs, Coalgate, or other communities, and the Italians sometimes enjoyed a night of opera together. Throughout the coal-mining towns Italian social organizations sponsored picnics on Sundays, and Italians from the area would gather to eat, sing, and play games. Two of the favorite games that originated in the old country that the Italians played were *morra* and *bocce*. *Morra* is played by two persons at a time using the fingers. Both players extend some of their fingers and say a number; the player who guesses the sum of the fingers is the winner. *Bocce* is a ball game played on a small dirt court and somewhat resembles bowling. *Bocce* became so popular in the area that tournaments were often held between various communities in the coal-mining district. Thus the games and reliable friends provided a sense of social autonomy and gave some semblance of the styles of living the Italians had enjoyed in the old country.

No matter how isolated the colonies of Italians became, it was impossible to escape entirely from the other people in the area. The men worked side by side with Americans, Lithuanians, Irishmen, Poles, and members of other nationalities. The children went to school with members of other nationalities. A catastrophe or strike often forced all to work together for a common goal. The mine explosion in Krebs in 1892, which took almost one hundred lives, caused Italians and other nationalities to work together to save the survivors and to share in the financial and moral support for the families of the victims. The prolonged strike that occurred between 1898 and 1903 joined Italians with other nationalities in bringing about the recognition of the union. Subsequent strikes and hardships brought the various groups together.

Several character traits attributed to many Italians in the coal-mining communities helped identify and describe their culture. Americans in Oklahoma, as well as throughout the United States, recognized in particular the frugality of the Italian immigrants. Coming

Kenny L. Brown

Competing *bocce* teams from Haileyville and Bache, at Haileyville in 1927. Courtesy of Mrs. Edith Hamilton.

from a country where opportunity and money were scarce, the Italians lived as thriftily as possible and saved as much money as they could. Rather than trust American bankers, many of the Italians in Oklahoma buried or hid their money, and families often had hundreds of dollars stashed in some unlikely spot. Around 1905 one resident of Krebs explained: "I will wager that here at Krebs there are at least fifty thousand dollars buried under ground; the workmen are justly afraid of the so-called bankers and prefer to hide their money."[3] In later years the Italians began trusting their savings to John B. Tua, the Italian consular agent for the state's coal-mining district; he in turn deposited their money. Some local banks eventually opened "Italian departments" headed by Italian leaders attempting to lure their countrymen's savings.

The reputation of thrift continued and the prestige of Italians increased in the area, though this frugality was sometimes used against them. For example, coal operators, when they wanted to demonstrate that wages were adequate, would emphasize that the Italians lived quite well on their incomes from mining. J. G. Puterbaugh, president of the McAlester Fuel Company, explained this to the Oklahoma Coal Strike Commission of 1919, which investigated the conditions of the coal-mining industry. He claimed that many of

49

the more ambitious Italian miners earned from $150 to $190 a month, living on half and saving about half. He further stated, "By this I want to make it clear that the man who is thrifty and who wants to work and wants a home and wants to save has the opportunity to do that in working in the mines on the present wage scale."[4] Such testimony during strikes usually resulted in blocking the miners in their attempt to increase wages.

Italians in Oklahoma used their savings in two major ways: they sent it back to Italy or they bought homes in the area. Because almost one-half of the Italian men were unmarried with families still living in Italy and because many returned home to visit each year, a large amount of the money went to relatives in the old country. The Italians sent more money abroad than any other immigrant group. The total from Krebs, McAlester, Alderson, and Coalgate in 1908 was estimated at over $100,000. Sometimes the money went with immigrants returning to Italy; at other times it was sent by mail to wives, mothers, and other relatives in the homeland. One tragic instance of sending money home involved an Italian killed at Krebs in the explosion of 1892. After his death the bloody, torn clothes of the unfortunate immigrant were draped across a fence. For a week no one took them until the dead man's brother arrived from the East. The brother claimed the clothes, searched them, and discovered $975 sewed inside. Adding twenty-five dollars of his own money, the man sent $1,000 to his mother in Italy.

The money-saving Italians also owned more land and homes than any other foreign group in the coal-mining region. If the Italians neither sent their savings home nor bought land in Oklahoma, they usually invested in their own grocery stores or purchased stock in local business. The thrift of the Italian immigrants aided in the development of the area as well as increasing their prestige in the community.

Italians also had a strong sense of honor. Often an agreement was sealed only with a handshake, and anyone who broke such an agreement was scorned. In one instance an Italian who had been betrayed by a fellow countryman became so incensed that he trailed him for 4,000 miles to get revenge. The odyssey began in the fall of 1902 when authorities in Indian Territory arrested Angelo Scalfia for illegally selling whiskey. After spending a month in jail, he asked Antonio Seguio, a businessman in South McAlester, to furnish $4,000 for bond. Seguio mortgaged his home to raise the money. After his release, Scalfia immediately disappeared, which meant that Seguio's money would be forfeited.

When he realized Scalfia had left, Seguio pursued him. For three months Seguio followed the fugitive from place to place until the chase ended in Chicago on December 27, 1902. On that day, Scalfia, weary from the ordeal and fearing for his life, surrendered to two detectives of the Chicago police force. If Scalfia had returned to Indian Territory within five days after his capture, the bond would have been saved; however, Seguio was not interested in the money—he wanted revenge. After the episode the dissatisfied Seguio explained: "I started to kill him, followed him for thousands of miles, and then at the last moment he escapes. It is hard. I would not have it so."[5] At least this one Italian in Oklahoma took seriously the keeping of a pledge.

One of the most important and familiar institutions for the Italians in Oklahoma was the Catholic church. In Oklahoma Italian participation and reaction to the church resembled many of the habits of the Catholics in Italy. Although Catholicism was the religion of an overwhelming majority of the citizens of Italy during the late nineteenth and early twentieth centuries, the active involvement of its believers was somewhat limited. Particularly in southern Italy, only the patron saints, holidays, and *festas* (festivals) were considered to be an important part of religious life. A number of women, children, and old men frequently attended church, but the younger men seldom became involved. Part of the problem was the priest, who many times was revered by some but not respected by the majority of the people. The peasants tended to associate the priest with the institutionalized church that at one time had been the largest landowner in Italy. The clergy often aligned themselves with the *signori* or upper class; as a result, their spiritual influence was never great with the people in Italy.

Many of the Italian immigrants brought this anticlerical attitude with them to America. The strong Irish influence in the American church further intensified the animosity of the Italians who resented the strange customs and ideas of the mainstream of Catholicism in the United States. Nevertheless, they still were baptized, married, and buried in the church. Also, they continued to revere their patron saints and participate in their festivals such as the Mt. Carmel Day celebration held annually on July 16.

In Indian Territory, Catholic churches were founded in the early

51

days of the coal-mining era. Dedicated and self-sacrificing Catholic ministers performed the first masses in the region. Throughout the nineteenth century these missionary priests from neighboring states had traveled through Indian Territory seeking converts among the Indians. Later, railroad workers, many of whom were Irish, attracted the attention of the priests when the Missouri, Kansas, and Texas Railroad was built through the area in 1872. In response primarily to the needs of those Irish laborers, a church was built at Atoka on the M. K. & T. Railroad, and in 1875 Father Isidore Robot, accompanied by Italian lay brother Dominic Lambert, became the first permanent priest for the church. Father Robot soon gained the position of "Prefect Apostolic of Indian Territory," and expanded his work through the area, establishing Sacred Heart Mission in present-day Pottawatomie County, Oklahoma, for the Indians.

While Father Robot was extending his services, Father Paul M. Ferroar Ponziglione, an Italian Jesuit, conducted missions to the mining camps near McAlester and Savanna. "Father Paul," as he was known, was the son of the Italian Count of Borgo d'Ales. He taught at a Jesuit College in Genoa, was captured there by Sardinian rebels in the revolution of 1848, and then went into exile as a missionary to the Osages, Chippewas, Cheyennes, and other Indians. In the 1870s and 1880s he made trips to several Indian Territory towns including McAlester and Savanna. There he conducted mass, performed other services, and prepared the way for permanent churches.

Much of Father Paul's work was completed by Father Robot, who left the Sacred Heart Mission to establish permanent residence in McAlester in October 1885. He and Brother Dominic built a small home that contained a room for services. They soon erected a small church for the Catholic miners of Savanna. At Krebs in 1886 they built a church, a two-room schoolhouse, and living quarters for several nuns.

Subsequently Catholic churches were established in other parts of the coal-mining district, serving Italians as well as other immigrants. Churches were built at Lehigh in 1887, Coalgate in 1890, Hartshorne in 1895, McAlester in 1896, Poteau in 1899, and Henryetta in 1908. Numerous other churches and missions served Catholics throughout the coalfields. Italian Catholics in these areas displayed characteristics similar to their countrymen in Italy. The men tended to regard the church as a place for women and children, and many of the men attended church only on special holidays. In some areas Italians were distressed and were hesitant to become involved in the church because there were no priests who knew their language and customs, a situation that caused a minor conflict between a priest in Krebs and his parishioners. In Pittsburg, where a majority of the Catholics were Mexicans, church officials classified many Italians as "fallen-away" Catholics. Nevertheless, the Italians used the church for religious services, baptisms, marriages, and funerals. Even with its weaknesses, the church remained the center of spiritual growth for many Italians who continued to consider themselves Catholics, and they gave freely to its causes. For instance, the natives of Castiglione di Carovilli who lived in Krebs in 1905 joined their friends in Hubbard, Ohio, and Brookside, Colorado, in donating several thousand dollars to build a new church for their hometown in Italy.

The Italian members of Saint Joseph's Church in Krebs were so numerous that they dominated the congregation, giving it the most distinctly Italian quality of any church in Oklahoma. Reflecting the Italian atmosphere was the annual church-related festival in honor of "Our Lady of Mt. Carmel." Held on July 16, the festival celebrated the miracle of Mt. Carmel, which occurred in 1251 when the Virgin Mary appeared to Simon Stock and presented him with the brown clothing later adopted by the Carmelite Order. The Roman Catholic Church approved the observance of this miracle in the fourteenth century and southern Italians began celebrating the event in the seventeenth century. For the southern Italian peasant, Mt. Carmel was not a solemn or austere occasion; it was a chance to escape from the drudgery of work with a boisterous festival. In the United States the Mt. Carmel celebration was the favorite of Italians. During the height of the immigration period, on every July 16, the "Little Italys" of the urban areas broke into merrymaking after priests performed the customary mass.

Although the number of participants was smaller than in the urban areas, the festivals sponsored by the church at Krebs were no less enthusiastic. The celebration was first held in 1893, a year after the *Congrega del Carmine* ("Carmelite Religious Guild") formed to organize the festivities. Mt. Carmel Day became a tradition over the years as it was sometimes expanded to two and three days of celebration. Hundreds of non-Italians and non-Catholics attended the festival, which was sometimes held in Sans Souci Park between McAlester and Krebs. The activities featured food, baseball, extravagant fireworks, and music. At no other time was the influence of the Italians so apparent.

Most Italians celebrated Mt. Carmel Day; yet many more had

more extensive contact with the church through the parochial schools. This was similar to the cities throughout the United States where the church provided education for Italian immigrants who could not attend the public schools. In Oklahoma, the church provided the only learning facilities available in some areas. Prior to statehood, some towns maintained schools by subscription, and coal operators provided some such services; however, the Choctaw government supported no schools for the whites. The only facilities available for many Italians in the territorial days were the Catholic schools, the first being established at Krebs on September 7, 1886. One year after its opening, 120 pupils attended Saint Joseph's School. Elsewhere parochial schools were later established in McAlester, Hartshorne, Henryetta, and other coal-mining towns. As free public schools opened after statehood, the importance of the Catholic institutions declined. Many Italians nevertheless continued to send their children to parochial schools, keeping this close tie with the church, until they closed in the 1960s.

Many Italians belonged to nonreligious organizations that were created strictly for Italians. These various societies were located in many towns in the coal-mining district: the *Fratellanza Indipendente* at Phillips, the *Fratellanza Minatori* and the *Menotti Garibaldi* at Coalgate, the *Fratellanza Lavoratori* at Lehigh, the *Dante Aligheri* at Dow, and both the *Stella d'Italia* and the *Cristoforo Colombo* at Krebs. Although these eventually became almost totally social and fraternal orders, in the early years most were mutual-aid societies that took care of their members in times of hardship. Their functions originally resembled labor organizations, as indicated by some of their titles — *Fratellanza Minatori* ("Fraternity of Miners") or *Fratellanza Lavoratori* ("Fraternity of Workers").

Italians in Oklahoma, and throughout the country, patterned their clubs after the "mutual-aid societies" in their homeland. In Italy these groups originally had been established by philanthropists who desired to teach the peasants thrift and self-reliance, thereby avoiding strikes and political upheaval. Ironically, the mutual-aid organizations did not remain apolitical; instead, they gradually developed into trade unions, some of them quite radical.

The first and by far the most active of the mutual-aid societies in Oklahoma was the *Cristoforo Colombo* ("Christopher Columbus") Society in Krebs. The society was formed by a group of northern Italians on May 18, 1881, after the need for group benefits became apparent. The Italian community consisted primarily of a floating

The Christopher Columbus Society's Italian band from Krebs, 1905. Courtesy of Johnnie Lalli.

population of men who were unmarried or who had no relatives in the area. When these men became ill, they usually had no one to provide for them, and the fact that they were missing work only added to their difficulties. Consequently, a number of these men formed the society, which they designed to provide insurance and sick benefits.

The charter members who established the organization wrote and published a large number of rules and guidelines for the members. Those who applied for membership in the organization had to meet several qualifications. Only men born in Italy or sons of Italian fathers could join, provided they spoke the Italian language. Membership was open to men between eighteen and fifty years of age who had been residents of Krebs for at least three months. If an applicant met all the requirements and was invited to join, he was then required to give background information on his life and to present a medical certificate to the members.

The society was financed by admission fees, monthly dues, contributions, and fines. Drawing from these revenues, the organization provided both sickness and death benefits. Five dollars per week was paid to those members who became ill. If the illness proved to be serious and involved a period of time longer than six months, the recipient was paid one-half of the weekly compensation. A permanent committee was assigned to visit sick members and to report on their condition to the society, and a doctor was designated for those members needing care. If a member died, his wife received forty dollars to pay expenses. If a member lost his wife— *"only by death not otherwise"*—he received twenty dollars.[6] If a funeral was near Krebs, the society accorded funeral honors with the participating members dressed in black military-like caps and sashes. Since the organization's concern was to provide for the members who needed aid, expulsion or fines were imposed on those who made fraudulent claims for benefits.

All of the functions of the society were not strictly businesslike. Authors of the constitution proclaimed that the club should "facilitate the relation among Italians as members of but one family." As a result the organization sponsored frequent social activities. This was true for all similar organizations in the coalfields of Oklahoma as well. Whether in Lehigh, Coalgate, or Krebs, the Italian men in the community joined their friends every Sunday at the local lodge hall to play cards or *bocce*. Often there were picnics or dances at the clubs, and several of the lodges sponsored extravagant Columbus Day celebrations in their communities. The Christopher Columbus Society supported a band, with its twenty-five members playing brass, stringed, and percussion instruments. The band played at various activities such as the Fourth of July and Columbus Day celebrations. In some instances the group assembled at mines when the workers went on strikes.

Whether they heard the band at celebrations, passed by when the members were playing *bocce* at a lodge, or saw one of the societies accord funeral honors, the citizens of the coal-mining communities were aware of the Italian organizations. Unlike their mutual-aid prototypes in Italy, they were not radical or political organizations. They met many of the economic and social needs of their members. Over the years, however, the membership declined and many Italians left for more prosperous places. Also the critical needs of the early days disappeared as the labor unions duplicated some of the needed functions and as the members became more self-sufficient. The Italians gradually turned away from their old clubs and joined American social and fraternal clubs. As early as 1911, for instance, an all-Italian lodge of the Order of Odd Fellows was formed at Alderson.

By the 1940s most of the original Italian societies ceased to exist with some consolidating with the Columbus lodge at Krebs. In recent years some of the old members of that group continued to meet informally in Krebs to play cards and relive old times.

Another cultural inclination that the Italians brought with them to Oklahoma was the dependency on one influential man in the community. The tendency for singular male authority was well-rooted in many Italians. The Italian family had a structure with male dominance; their religion had priests with absolute authority; the large plantation-like Italian farms had landlords with unlimited power; and, in America, many Italian communities had *padroni* with strong influence. *Padroni* were Italian men who were particularly influential in the early days of immigration when there were no restrictions on contract labor. Often working as a foreman at a nearby industry, a *padrone* used his influence to find jobs for newcomers, charging a fee for his services and making large profits from the unwitting Italian immigrant. In cooperation with similar agents in Italy, these opportunists were instrumental in obtaining laborers who received steamship fare to be repaid with a large interest after arrival. The Foran Act of 1885 and similar legislation in Italy, however, outlawed the practice of this contract labor. The *padroni* decreased in power, giving way to respectable leaders who handled the affairs of the Italian immigrants. Many of these new leaders were reformed *padroni,* yet others were simply men of ability who filled the much-needed role. Sometimes they became consultants for the Italians on legal and social matters. They charged fees for their services or benefited indirectly for their leadership. Often these leaders were still called *padroni,* but they were much less corrupt and frequently very helpful to the Italians.

Oklahoma was relatively free of any unethical influence of the *padroni;* however, there were *padrone*-like leaders in many communities. At Fort Cobb many of the Italians looked to Antonio Caruso for guidance; in fact, many had followed him there. Italian men of influence in Coalgate were Giovanni Gentilini and Pasquale Ferrero, owners of local stores. At Wilburton such men as the grocer Luigi Antonelli guided many Italians. And at Krebs and McAlester Giuseppe Fassino and his brother Giovanni helped many of their compatriots make decisions in the early days. But the most influential of all Italian leaders in Oklahoma was Giovanni B. Tua.

Tua became a guiding force for the Italians throughout the coalfields of Oklahoma particularly during the first quarter of the twentieth century. He was born in Marseilles, France, on November 18, 1871. His parents had immigrated to France much like many other northern Italians in the early stages of emigration. He was educated in France and Italy and could speak fluently the languages of both countries, a skill that later aided him in his position as consular agent for the coal-mining region of Oklahoma. In 1891, Tua left Italy to join two sisters of his in Osage City, Kansas, where he worked as a coal miner. After moving to Missouri and Texas, he migrated to Hartshorne on November 1, 1896. He labored for a year in a cement plant there, then moved to McAlester to work in the new macaroni factory owned by Joe and John Fassino. Again he soon changed employment, opening a confectionary and fruit business in McAlester. Later Tua established a restaurant where he enjoyed a good business until 1910, then devoted his full time to his position as Royal Italian Consular Agent for Oklahoma. Joe Fassino had held the title for a number of years previously but quit because of his thriving partnership in the macaroni factory.

Tua did not receive official sanction as Royal Italian Consular Agent until 1910; nevertheless, he carried out many of the duties several years prior to gaining his title. In 1902 the *Muskogee Phoenix*, referring to him as a *padrone*, explained: "Interpreter, restaurateur, banker, immigration agent, steamship agent, foreign-exchange agent, Italian consul, this man is a power in the mining district. He is more powerful even than the president of the coal trust in the mining district because he could cause every one of the Italian miners to walk out of the mines indefinitely if he wanted to."[7] The newspaper also said that, as banker for the Italians, he had to carry large sums of cash with him and often would sit in his restaurant all night with $20,000 on his person. Allegedly Tua had access to $250,000 which he had in his name at a local bank.

Although the *Muskogee Phoenix* exaggerated Tua's importance as well as his bankroll, he was the most influential Italian in the coal-mining region. He was generally conservative in philosophy and used his influence to moderate any radical tendencies he saw in his fellow countrymen. In the role of Italian consular agent, his duties were varied. He often transacted much business for Italians in Oklahoma with their fellow countrymen at Tontitown, Arkansas; Montague, Texas; Pittsburg, Kansas; and other communities in adjacent states. He attended to writing wills, recording land transactions, and exchanging foreign currency. Because he issued passports, he conveniently became steamship agent for the numerous Italians who traveled to and from their old country. These duties also brought him into contact with other nationalities for whom he transacted business as well. This position gave him enormous influence in the community; however, it did not go uncontested. In 1914 another Italian in the area had charges brought against Tua in an attempt to oust him as consular agent. The accuser, evidently wanting some of the power for himself, claimed that Tua had charged fees as a paid witness in certain court cases and naturalization hearings. The State Department temporarily withdrew its recognition of Tua as consular agent when charges were brought against him. Numerous very prominent men in the community came to Tua's aid by signing affidavits that were sent to the State Department attesting to the good character of Tua. After a complete investigation the indictment was quickly dropped. Tua soon regained his title of Consular Agent and con-

John B. Tua, consular agent and leader among the Italians in Oklahoma, in his office in McAlester. Courtesy of Bert Tua and the *McAlester News-Capital.*

tinued serving the Italian community in that capacity until 1941 when the United States broke diplomatic relations with Italy.

From 1941 to 1959, Tua operated a tourist and foreign-exchange agency, along with a growing interest in real estate transactions. Many first-generation Italians still sought his services in legal matters even though the consular agency was officially closed. He died on February 24, 1960. Tua had represented the American manifestation of an Italian characteristic—the tendency to depend on a strong male authority. He also had served as an aide to thousands of Italians in the area. When he was forced to retire from the consular service, and in the years that followed, the Italian-Americans had been assimilated in the ways, languages, and customs of their new homes. He had continued to aid many Italians, but his later influence had slowly decreased in comparison to his early leadership.

The Italian social structure and web of cultural institutions had tensions that were transplanted to Oklahoma. In Italy, northern Italians generally considered their compatriots in the southern regions inferior and uncultured. In Oklahoma, the same attitude prevailed and the two groups of Italians stayed apart. Even some of the social organizations, such as the Christopher Columbus Society, initially were open only to northern Italians. In some coal-mining communities, the two groups of Italians lived together if the total Italian population was small. They divided into separate colonies if a large number of both northern and southern Italians lived in the same town. In most instances, the northern Italians tolerated their southern countrymen, but a number of the hostilities of the old country were apparent between the two factions in Oklahoma. Over time much of the animosity between the groups vanished. Yet even in recent years many old attitudes have been apparent as some northern Italians of the first or second generations seem quick to identify themselves as "northern" rather than "southern" Italians.

Not only the prejudices but also the real inequities of the southern problem accompanied the Italians to the coal-mining area of Oklahoma. The southern Italians had fewer educational opportunities in Italy and were less able to deal with the language and customs of their new homes. A survey of a number of immigrants in Kansas and Oklahoma in 1911 indicated that over 80 percent of the Italians from northern Italy could read and write while only about 60 percent of the Italians from southern Italy were literate. As a result, many of the southern Italians were slower to learn English, even those who had been in the country from fifteen to twenty years. They also had some of the same attitudes that had been apparent in their isolated village in Italy. In their old homes they distrusted anyone from outside the hamlet. In the coalfields they lived in colonies, seldom associated with natives, and showed little interest outside their own immediate neighborhood. Many of the southern Italians also refused to encourage their children to attend school or to speak English. The northern Italians, on the other hand, grasped American customs more quickly and learned English more easily. These abilities in turn resulted in a greater interest in affairs of the community and a stronger inclination to settle permanently in the region.

Many Americans held the same prejudices and recognized distinctions between the two groups of Italians living in the various coal-mining communities of Oklahoma. Residents considered the southern Italians backward, clannish, and inferior to the northern Italians. Law enforcement officers believed that the southern Italians were prone to criminality. Conversely, natives held the northern Italians in higher esteem, largely because of their inclination to become Americanized more quickly.

Ironically even the northern Italians did not escape prejudicial attitudes as many people simply spoke of Italians as only one group. The Italians as a whole were subject to a caste system that placed Americans and British immigrants above them but other immigrant groups below them. In the coal mines the hierarchical system was apparent. Few native-born Americans worked with any foreigners except for immigrants from the British Isles. Some of the laborers, such as drivers and trackmen, worked more under the direction of the company and were placed side-by-side with people of different nationalities.

Outside of the mines in the various communities Italians were generally treated fairly. In some situations, however, native-born Americans occasionally insulted Italians by calling them "wops" and "dagos" or otherwise mistreating them. During the 1920s some local Ku Klux Klan organizations harassed the Italians to a small degree in a few communities. Minor threats and taunts from the Klan were probably directed at the Italians as much for their Catholic affiliation as for their foreign birth. The same general intemperate atmosphere that gave rise to the Klan generally affected many people during the 1920s. A typical attitude is reflected in a statement taken in 1929 from a student at the University of Oklahoma who said: "They [the Italians and other foreigners] do not Americanize easily. They care nothing about progress. All they desire are dollars with which to go back to the old country and live a life of leisure. They drink enormously and are highly excitable."⁸ Not everyone had such opinions, but they were all too frequent. Most prejudicial attitudes disappeared in the years that followed as the old Italian immigrants became more and more respected for their accomplishments.

The most harmful stereotype to the Italians was the belief that the *mafia* or other such violent organizations were a part of the lives of virtually every Italian immigrant. Such notions were not realistic. Violent clandestine elements existed and terrorized Italians and other groups, but the extent of their actions was limited and was found almost exclusively in urban areas. In Oklahoma violent activities occurred only in 1909 when violence erupted in Krebs. It was extremely rare, involving a "Black Hand" group composed of three Italians. The Black Hand was a prototype of the more powerful *mafia* groups in the early 1900s. The Black Hand Societies (as well as the old and present-day *mafia*) were not formal or well-defined organizations. They were unrelated criminal gangs that sought to control others and profit by using violence. They usually threatened other Italians and signed their extortionate demands with a small figure of a black hand.

In the series of events involving the Black Hand in Krebs, at least three men tried to blackmail prominent citizens of Krebs in 1909. The conspirators had repeatedly threatened Joe Nellis, a store owner in the small town, warning that they would kill him if he did not pay them $1,000. Nellis refused, and his store was dynamited at 1:00 A.M. on March 31, 1909. A few days later, Nellis received another note that ordered him to place $1,000 in a coke oven at the Degnan and McConnel plant at nearby Alderson. Nellis notified the sheriff who sent two deputies to take care of the matter. Concealing themselves in a small shack, they pounced on a man when he attempted to retrieve Nellis' ransom from the coke oven. Three other Italians were later arrested, and it was discovered that they had ties with others near Chicago. An interstate conspiracy was suspected but never proved. Three of the men involved, all Sicilians, later were indicted. But the fourth person arrested, a "northern Italian lad," was released after authorities had determined that he was not a part of the blackmailing scheme.

Evidently the desire to make easy money became contagious, for within a few days Joe Lardi of Hartshorne was arrested for attempting to extort $1,000 from J. H. Baker, a merchant and vice-president of the First State Bank of Hartshorne. Perhaps Lardi had heard of the schemes of the Black Hand in Krebs and decided to try extortion for himself. He had resided in Hartshorne for several months where he became acquainted with Baker and knew that the banker-merchant was relatively wealthy. His plan failed. Local authorities used the same tactics that the deputies had used in Krebs, catching Lardi in the act of picking up the money on April 8, 1909.[9]

The episodes of the Black Hand in Krebs and Hartshorne were unique. They were striking exceptions to the usually peaceful atmosphere of the Italian communities. This was different from many areas in Sicily where the *mafia*, which using similar tactics, grew into a political and social tool. Also the inability of the Black Hand to operate effectively contrasts greatly with several large American cities where the neighborhood Black Hand groups thrived and eventually consolidated as part of the American *mafia*. Consequently, the indignation of the people in Oklahoma against the violent tactics of a handful of conspirators showed that criminal actions would not be tolerated in the area. The Black Hand could find no foothold in Oklahoma.

One cultural tradition, the drinking of intoxicating beverages,

Italians from the Hartshorne-Haileyville area about 1910, enjoying "Choc" beer. Left to right: Joe Luciano, Dominic Clemente, Dan Rigazzi, Eli Gizzi, and Angelo Centello. Courtesy of Mrs. Dan Rigazzi, Jr.

became a constant source of conflict between the Italians and law enforcement officials in the coal-mining communities. From the early days of mining, the Italians and other immigrants made illegal whiskey and beer for their own use as well as for sale. The favorite homemade brew of most miners was "Choctaw" or "Choc" beer which was made from barley, hops, tobacco, fishberries, and a small amount of alcohol. Many Italian women made and sold the "Choc" beer to supplement the family income. Indian agent D. M. Wisdom complained of the situation, explaining that medical explanations often were used to justify the illegal manufacture and use of the "Choc" beer and whiskey: "Many miners insist it is essential to their health, owing to the bad water usually found in mining camps, and they aver they use it rather as a tonic or medicine than as a beverage, and this idea, that it is a proper tonic is fostered and encouraged by some physicians." Wisdom explained that it was a mystery to the scientific world that "the water is always bad in the immediate mining centers, but good in the adjacent neighborhoods."[10]

Prohibition remained in effect in the Choctaw Nation throughout territorial days, and the Italians continued to violate the law. Shortly before statehood several miners in the area of McAlester and Krebs complained about the restrictions on drinking. They explained that the strenuous work in the mines caused great fatigue and also argued that the air in the mines was often extremely hot and vitiated by the gas escaping from the coal seams. As a result, when they left their work in the evening, they "needed something to drink stronger than water in order to catch their breath." One Italian miner who had lived elsewhere in the world explained: "I worked for years in Asia Minor; notwithstanding that the Koran strictly forbids to Mohammedans the use of spirituous drinks, the Turks allowed us Christians to drink wine, beer and other liquors at our pleasure."[11]

Because the constitution and a prohibition law were passed simultaneously in 1907, statehood brought no relief to the Italians and other immigrants in the coal-mining communities of Oklahoma. In 1908, about 30 percent of the indictments for illegal use of intoxicants were issued against foreigners in the three principal coal-mining counties. Italians were charged on approximately 20 percent of the total charges. Between 1907 and 1930 a large majority of the criminal charges against Italians involved an unlawful use or sale of alcoholic beverages. Most of these violations were minor since many of the Italians simply drank with family and friends or sold liquor to people in the community. Nevertheless, Krebs and other towns with large Italian populations gained notoriety for lawlessness and bootlegging.

Those who wished to cast doubt on the character of Italians in the area often pointed to the illicit manufacture of wine, whiskey, and "Choc" beer. For instance, Lieutenant J. H. Carey, regimental intelligence officer for the Oklahoma National Guard stationed in the area during the strike of 1919, issued secret reports that went first to his commanding officer then to Governor J. B. A. Robertson. Governor Robertson, influenced by the national hysteria known as the Red Scare and fearing that radicals and Bolsheviks might be in the coal-mining districts, probably expected that Lieutenant Carey would find many such culprits in the area. Carey, straining to reveal evidence of radicalism to his superiors, reported that an Italian was involved in illicit activities. He wrote: "Tony Petitti is running a bootlegging joint wide open (practically) near Hartshorne, selling corn whiskey and Choc."[12] In the same report he revealed that an Italian woman was making "Choc" beer for agitators who met secretly on a hill near Hartshorne. Thus when few clues of Bolshevism could be found, the officer grasped for any type of illegal activity he could find.

Although many people had negative opinions about the manufacture of liquor and beer in the coal-mining communities, the Italians and others continued to produce their homemade brews throughout the 1920s. The bad reputation of many towns became widespread. For instance, because Krebs had a reputation of bootlegging and other illegal pursuits, some people from other cities in the state would smile condescendingly when they heard the word "Krebs." This image of lawlessness led to an investigation of the town. Early in 1928 authorities revealed that John Oxford, a resident of Krebs who had been arrested for murder, owned a secret gambling house in the small town. Governor Henry S. Johnston, a man quickly appalled by such immorality, responded immediately by calling for a formal inquiry concerning Krebs. W. E. Gotcher, Pittsburg County Attorney, led the ensuing investigation, bringing before him the city commission and law enforcement officials of Krebs. In his report to Oklahoma Attorney General Edwin Dabney, Gotcher admitted that the problem had existed for years and that it was caused partially by the estimated 1,500 Italians who lived in Krebs at the time. Gotcher explained, "We have had some trouble there due to the fact that some Italians and a few other foreigners and Americans persist in keeping Choctaw beer for their own use and selling it to the public in general."[13] Tom Caswell, the chief of police of Krebs, further conceded that the largest number of Italians kept Choctaw beer for their own use and that some sold it for twenty-five cents a quart. Even with this damaging testimony, however, Attorney General Dabney reported favorably to the governor on the situation in Krebs, saying that the city officials of Krebs did not license any place to operate gambling dens or saloons and that the town did not have such establishments other than the one owned by Oxford. Dabney further added that the general moral condition of Krebs compared favorably with the other communities.

The special inquiry of 1928 did little to change the habits of the citizens of Krebs or other mining communities in Oklahoma. In fact, the depression years that followed caused the manufacture and sale of "Choc" beer and whiskey to flourish. Many Italians created an income by making "Choc" beer. Even after the repeal of prohibition in 1959, a customer could buy "Choc" beer in Krebs simply by asking some of the right people in the town.

Chapter 5

RECENT EVENTS AND TRENDS

Distinctly Italian character traits and social institutions were well known in the coal-mining communities of Oklahoma. Gradually this Italian influence weakened as the Italian population decreased, thus forcing Italians to amalgamate with the larger society that surrounded them. Poor economic conditions and the end of immigration caused the decline in the Italian population in the state. As early as the decade of 1910 to 1920, the fluctuations of the coal-mining industry had a discernible impact. In 1910 the number of Italians was 2,226 in the four principal coal-mining counties. By 1920 they numbered 1,827—a decrease of 399 or almost 18 percent. In addition to out-migrations that caused the reduction, there were internal fluctuations within the four counties. This was because of the depletion of old mines in some areas or the development of new mines in other locations. The number of Italians decreased in Pittsburg and Coal counties where the old mines were playing out, but increased in Latimer and Okmulgee counties, the latter more than tripling its Italian population. An increase in production during World War I resulted in better wages and more days of employment for the coal miners in all areas; however, during the 1920s the industry declined to the point of economic disaster for both the workers and the operators. Competition with fuel oil and natural gas forced the owners to lower prices and wages, which, in turn, caused the prolonged strike of 1924–27. The union could not avoid a cut in wages, and violence erupted when operators brought in strikebreakers. The union workers lost. This unfortunate situation of the 1920s destroyed the union, bankrupted many coal companies, and reduced the coal-mining communities to decaying towns.

The poor economic conditions and the strike ironically aided the status of Italians and other foreigners at the expense of the British and American miners. The overabundance of workers and competition for employment had an equalizing effect that destroyed much of the old caste system of the coalfields. The once-superior American and British miners lost prestige and no longer held favorable positions with the operators. They had dominated the union in the past and used it in maintaining their power base. But during the strike of 1924–27 the mine owners brought in strikebreakers, and the union failed to function successfully. The skilled miners were reduced to laboring side-by-side with inexperienced workers and, worse yet, with scabs. This circumstance destroyed old barriers and brought about a general acceptance of all groups in the coal fields, except for blacks and some farmers who worked as strikebreakers. As a result, the southern and eastern Europeans, including the Italians, became a component part of the communities in the coalfields and were even socially acceptable to the British and American miners. The once-criticized differences in culture were accounted for with the reasoning that "he is an Italian, but a good fellow just the same."[1]

During the disastrous times between 1920 and 1930, many Italians left the Oklahoma coalfields, ironically for the same reason they had immigrated from Italy—because of economic turmoil. Within the decade almost 1,000 foreign-born Italians moved from the four principal counties. They were not the only group affected. While Okmulgee County showed a slight increase, the entire population decreased significantly in three of the counties. In comparison to the total reduction of population, the percentage of Italians who left the area was quite high. Between 1920 and 1930 the overall population of Pittsburg County decreased only about 3.5 percent whereas the Italian population in the same county declined approximately 40 percent. The total reduction of the general population for the county was 1,792 of which 426 were Italians. Although they made up only 2 percent of the population, they accounted for over 20 percent of the total loss. Other mining counties showed similar decreases.

Many of these Italians were going to more industrialized states. Over 200 left Krebs and went to work in the rubber industries of Akron and Toledo, Ohio. Italians from Krebs and other Oklahoma communities sought employment in the automobile industries of Detroit, Michigan, or in the diversified economies of California and Pennsylvania. Many moved within Oklahoma itself, working in the oil industry or in factories in the urban areas.

In the 1930s, 1940s, and afterward, the Italian population decreased rapidly in the old coal-mining counties. By 1970 first- and

FOREIGN-BORN ITALIANS IN OKLAHOMA
1910–1940

	1910	1920	1930	1940
Important Coal Mining Counties				
Coal	443	353	136	97
Latimer	321	353	102	70
Okmulgee	64	209	163	131
Pittsburg	1,398	912	486	359
Urban Counties				
Oklahoma	41	54	51	53
Tulsa	12	29	76	55
All Other Counties	285	212	143	128
State Totals	2,564	2,122	1,157	893

	1950	1960	1970
Recent State Totals	805	710	539

Source: Various tables from the *Population* volumes of the decennial census reports published by U.S. Bureau of the Census, 1910–1970.

second-generation Italians numbered only 60 in Coal County, 21 in Latimer County, 166 in Okmulgee County, and 575 in Pittsburg County. Statewide the total of first-generation Italians likewise decreased with only 539 listed in 1970.

Despite the decreasing number of foreign-born Italians and their second-generation offspring in the coal-mining counties, the total Italian foreign stock has remained steady statewide. In the last few decades the total was slightly increased with 3,531 listed in 1970, most of those being second-generation Italians. The main difference is that the majority of these now live in urban areas. Communities such as Lawton, Bartlesville, Muskogee, Stillwater, and Shawnee, have Italians of foreign stock, totaling thirty to fifty or more. The number of these Italian inhabitants in those cities equals or even surpasses the Italian population of the old coal-mining towns such as Wilburton or Coalgate. Similar to other Oklahomans, jobs have attracted these Italians to the cities over the years. They work in meat-packing plants, petroleum refineries, electronics firms, restaurants, and in many other businesses, both large and small.

In 1970 both the Tulsa and Oklahoma City metropolitan areas had more first- and second-generation Italians than any other counties, including Pittsburg County. This trend of settling in the urban areas is not, of course, a uniquely Italian phenomenon. It is part of a general pattern of urbanization among all people in Oklahoma. It also represents the attraction of Oklahoma as a "sunbelt" state, because many of the Italians of foreign stock in cities of Oklahoma have come from urban regions in Ohio, Pennsylvania, New York, and other northern states.

Like the urban Italians of foreign stock, the first- and second-generation Italians in the coal-mining counties have worked at a variety of occupations. A few continued to work in the coal mines, which operated periodically until the 1960s. Now the Italians of various generations in the area are ranchers, storekeepers, mechanics, restaurateurs, and factory workers. Most traces of the culture have disappeared, and they are recognized as being Italian by name only.

This assimilation, now so apparent in the coal-mining counties, was inevitable. The decline in the Italian population accelerated the process of assimilation. With so few of their countrymen in the region, the Italians were forced to form an increasing number of friendships and associations with people outside of their own nationality. Also out of necessity, many undertook occupations other than mining. This increased the number of acquaintances with non-Italians and gave the Italians firsthand knowledge of a variety of American business practices. Always small in numbers, the Italians of Oklahoma faced a much larger culture that required conformity. Once the Italians compromised with such pressure, the deterioration of their culture began. A vacuum was created that could only be filled by accepting new ways.

One of the vestiges of the old Italian-American culture in Oklahoma that remains is the language. Yet it is hardly recognizable. Many of the old immigrants spoke only Italian when they first arrived, and eventually they learned to speak a broken English. In recent years their English has improved, but their Italian has become faulty and barely comprehensible. Likewise the Catholic church in most areas can be identified only marginally as Italian. Perhaps the strongest tie to the past for the Italians is food. The families continue to serve the traditional dishes, and several famous restaurants offer fine Italian meals to the public. In all, few overt traces remain of the customs and institutions of the Italian immigrants in the Oklahoma coal-mining counties.

With so little of the culture left and with the processes of assimilation so complete, many Oklahomans of Italian descent are reviving and celebrating the old customs. In the urban areas of Oklahoma many newcomers to the state who are of Italian descent have joined with some of the former residents of the old coal-mining communities to form Italian clubs. In Norman in 1978 a group of second-generation and third-generation Italians established a local chapter of the Order of the Sons of Italy in America. This lodge is fashioned somewhat after the old fraternal and mutual-aid societies of the past. It is primarily a charitable and fraternal organization. Also in 1978 the American-Italian Club of Tulsa was founded. Not affiliated with any national group, this organization was established as a totally social club. Its goal is simply to preserve the Italian language and customs in Oklahoma. In addition to monthly meetings, the club sponsors holiday celebrations including a Christopher Columbus Day celebration. The Italian immigrants and their descendants in the old coal-mining district likewise have made recent efforts to preserve and celebrate their past. In 1971 the first annual Italian Festival was held at McAlester. Since then it has been held every year with the participants and spectators celebrating the culture and lives of the early-day Italian immigrants. Included are songs, dances, the *Re* and *Regina* (King and Queen), *bocce*, *morra*, and Italian food. In 1976 Saint Joseph's Church in Krebs celebrated the ninetieth anniversary of its founding. Participants temporarily relived the culture and color of the Italian parishioners. Appropriately held on July 18, the Sunday after Mt. Carmel Day, this celebration included a small-scale revival of the Mt. Carmel festival. Those who took part reminisced of old Italian institutions such as the Christopher Columbus Society, and they remembered the old days when Italian immigrants were numerous. Since 1976 the observance has once again become an annual event as part of the church's agenda.

The recent attempts to preserve the Italian culture in Oklahoma are commendable. The heritage of the Italians in Oklahoma is worthy of much study and celebration. After all, the Italian immigrants in the state faced many difficult challenges and made many contributions. They found an unusual social and legal situation in Indian Territory, which was different from any other area. Yet the Italians overcame the difficulties that arose from this circumstance, and eventually assimilated into the society of Oklahoma.

BIBLIOGRAPHICAL ESSAY

Although very little has been written about the Italians in Oklahoma, a great deal of information has been published on the Italians in the United States. Several historical and sociological studies give extensive details on the Italian-American experience. A few of these are Joseph Lopreato, *Italian Americans* (New York: Random House, Inc., 1970); Silvano M. Tomasi and Madeline H. Engels, eds. *The Italian Experience in the United States* (New York: Center for Migration Studies, Inc., 1970); and, still useful, Eliot Lord, John J. D. Trenor, and Samuel J. Barrows, *The Italian in American* (New York: B. F. Buck, 1905).

A particularly useful and enjoyable work for the general reader is Lawrence F. Pisani, *The Italian in America: A Social Study and History* (New York: Exposition Press, 1957). A study that has provoked more discussion than most is Nathan Glazer and D. P. Moynihan, *Beyond the Melting Pot: The Negroes, Puerto Ricans, Jews, Italians, and Irish in New York City* (Cambridge: Massachusetts Institute of Technology Press, 1970). The section in that book that deals with Italians should be read.

Very few of the more general works discuss Oklahoma to any great extent. The 1906 study by Lord, already mentioned, includes a few pages of details which are quite useful. Lord's description is summarized in Andrew F. Rolle, *The Immigrant Upraised: Italian Adventurers and Colonists in an Expanding America* (Norman: University of Oklahoma Press, 1968). Rolle's history is helpful in understanding how Oklahoma compares to other states west of the Mississippi River.

The most valuable and extensive coverage of the coalfields of Oklahoma appears in Frederick Ryan, *The Rehabilitation of the Oklahoma Coal Mining Communities* (Norman: University of Oklahoma Press, 1935). Although that work is dated, it gives much insight into the coal industry and includes some references to Italians and other groups. Similar coverage of the Italians is found in Gene

Aldrich, "A History of the Coal Industry in Oklahoma to 1907" (Ph.D. diss., University of Oklahoma, 1952). The chapters on the social and cultural aspects are particularly enjoyable. Much of the information that Ryan and Aldrich present is duplicated in two articles: Philip A. Kalisch, "Ordeal of the Oklahoma Coal Miners," *The Chronicles of Oklahoma* 48 (Autumn 1970): 331–40; and Stanley Clark, "Immigrants in the Choctaw Coal Industry," *The Chronicles of Oklahoma* 33 (Winter 1955–56): 440–55.

In addition to the coal-mining industry, the student of the Italian experience in Oklahoma should consult other topics. Angie Debo, *The Rise and Fall of the Choctaw Republic* (Norman: University of Oklahoma Press, 1934), is a good starting point. It is essential for the understanding of the political and social situation the Italians encountered in the Oklahoma coalfields. Oklahoma socialism is discussed in Garin Burbank, *When Farmers Voted Red: The Gospel of Socialism in the Oklahoma Countryside, 1910–1924* (Westport, Conn.: Greenwood Press, 1976). A more easily digestible work is the autobiography of the state's chief socialist organizer, Oscar Ameringer, *If You Don't Weaken* (New York: Henry Holt, 1940). Ameringer colorfully describes the conditions that fostered the strong Socialist party in Oklahoma with some discussion of the coal-mining areas. Clyde Hamm, ed., *Labor History of Oklahoma* (Oklahoma City: A. M. Van Horn, 1939), gives a good summary of the coal-mining unions.

Only two studies specifically cover the Italians in Oklahoma: Kenny L. Brown, "Peaceful Progress: A History of the Italians of Krebs, Oklahoma," *The Chronicles of Oklahoma* 53 (Fall 1975): 332–52; and, by the same author, "A History of the Italians in Pittsburg County, Oklahoma" (Master's thesis, Oklahoma State University, 1975). Virtually all of the information in those two works is included in this study.

Probably the best way to investigate the Italian experience in Oklahoma is to actually visit the old areas where the immigrants were numerous. This offers an excuse to visit some of the fine Italian restaurants in the area. A particularly good time to visit is during the Italian Festival, held annually just east of McAlester. For information, write the McAlester Chamber of Commerce, McAlester, Oklahoma, 74501.

NOTES

CHAPTER 1

1. For a discussion of the thorough assimilation process in the American West and its impact on Italian immigrants, see Andrew F. Rolle, *The Immigrant Upraised: Italian Adventurers and Colonists in an Expanding America* (Norman: University of Oklahoma Press, 1968).

2. Concerning the *Risorgimento* and the history of modern Italy, see Arthur James Whyte, *The Evolution of Modern Italy* (London: Basil Blackwell and Mott Ltd., 1959); Salvatore Saladino, *Italy from Unification to 1919: Growth and Decay of a Liberal Regime* (New York: Thomas Y. Crowell Company, 1970); Denis Mack Smith, *Italy: A Modern History* (Ann Arbor: University of Michigan Press, 1969); and Christopher Seton-Watson, *Italy from Liberalism to Fascism, 1870-1925* (London: Methuen and Company, Ltd., 1967).

3. See Shepard B. Clough, *The Economic History of Modern Italy* (New York: Columbia University Press, 1964).

4. Mack Smith, *Italy*, p. 242.

5. For general discussions of Italian immigration to the United States, see Joseph Lopreato, *Italian Americans* (New York: Random House, Inc., 1970); Lawrence Frank Pisani, *The Italian in America: A Social Study and History* (New York: Exposition Press, 1957); or Eliot Lord, John J. D. Trenor, and Samuel J. Barrows, *The Italian in America* (New York: B. F. Buck and Company, 1906).

CHAPTER 2

1. In the 1910 census, the American-born Italians with "both parents born in Italy" numbered 1,303. Added to the foreign-born Italians, the total becomes 3,867. This new figure is a better representation of the total number of Italians, although it does not include all Italians of foreign stock.

2. McAlester's own description of these events appears in James B. Thoburn and Muriel H. Wright, *Oklahoma: A History of the State and Its People*, 4 vols. (New York: Lewis Historical Publishing Company, Inc., 1929), vol. 2, pp. 879-80.

3. The composition of several coal-mining towns are given in U.S. Congress, Senate, *Reports of the Immigration Commission*, vol. 7: *Immigrants in Industries*, part 1: *Bituminous Coal Mining*, S. Doc. 633, 61st Cong., 3rd sess., 1911, pp. 19-25 (hereafter referred to as *Bituminous Coal Mining*).

4. Information on the trends of Italian immigration in Oklahoma and the places of origin came from the following sources: baptismal, marriage, and interment records at St. Joseph's Catholic Church, Krebs, Oklahoma, and at Blessed Sacrament Church, Coalgate, Oklahoma; naturalization records, Office of the Court Clerk, Pittsburg County Courthouse, McAlester, Oklahoma. Naturalization records, Office of the Court Clerk, Latimer County Courthouse, Wilburton, Oklahoma; and *Bituminous Coal Mining*, pp. 19–25.

5. These coal-mining counties included Haskell with twenty-six, LeFlore with eighteen, and Sequoyah with eleven foreign-born Italians.

6. The census for 1910 lists 78 Italians in McClain County in central Oklahoma. The naturalization records at the county courthouse and various records at Our Lady of Victory Catholic Church reveal no evidence of permanent residence. In addition, no second-generation Italians were listed in the census, which indicates these were migrant workers or the census listing is in error.

CHAPTER 3

1. For the most detailed histories of Oklahoma coal mining, see Frederick Ryan, *The Rehabilitation of Oklahoma Coal Mining Communities* (Norman: University of Oklahoma Press, 1935); and Gene Aldrich, "A History of the Coal Industry in Oklahoma to 1907" (Ph.D. diss., University of Oklahoma, 1952).

2. Norman Yoss, "Explosion at No. 11, Krebs," Coal-Mining File, Vertical Files, Oklahoma Historical Society, Oklahoma City, Oklahoma, p. 2.

3. On miners' unions in Oklahoma, see Ryan, *The Rehabilitation of Oklahoma Coal Mining Communities;* and Clyde Hamm, ed., *Labor History of Oklahoma* (Oklahoma City: A. M. Van Horn, 1939).

4. Louis Thompson to Samuel Boydston, February 13, 1921, Correspondence Files, Samuel Boydston Collection, Western History Collections, Bizzell Memorial Library, University of Oklahoma, Norman, Oklahoma.

5. Dominic Testa to Samuel Boydston, n.d. (c. 1916–19), Correspondence Files, Samuel Boydston Collection, Western History Collections, Bizzell Memorial Library, University of Oklahoma, Norman, Oklahoma.

6. On socialism and radical political movements in Italy, see Wayland Hilton-Young, *The Italian Left: A Short History of Political Socialism in Italy* (London: Longmans, Green, and Company, 1949); and Richard Hostetter, *The Italian Socialist Movement* (Princeton: Princeton University Press, 1958).

7. Socialism in Oklahoma is covered in detail in Howard L. Meredith, "A History of the Socialist Party in Oklahoma" (Ph.D. diss., University of Oklahoma, 1969); and Garin Burbank, *When Farmers Voted Red: The Gospel of Socialism in the Oklahoma Countryside, 1910–1924* (Westport, Conn.: Greenwood Press, 1976).

8. *South McAlester Capital,* May 20, 1897, p. 1.

9. Lord, *The Italian in America,* p. 108.

10. Interview with Carmine Finamore, Krebs, Oklahoma, March 17, 1979.

CHAPTER 4

1. The best written descriptions of the experiences of Italian women and families are found in *Bituminous Coal Mining*, pp. 38–59, 93–121. Additional information was taken from interviews with Maria Finamore, Krebs, Oklahoma, March 17, 1979; and an interview with Minnie Cioni, Krebs, Oklahoma, March 15, 1979.

2. Interview with Maria Finamore.

3. Lord, *The Italian in America*, p. 110.

4. Testimony of J. G. Puterbaugh, November 21, 1919, in "Record of the Coal Strike Commission," Governor J. B. A. Robertson Files, Oklahoma State Archives, Oklahoma City, Oklahoma.

5. *The Cherokee Advocate* (Tahlequah, Oklahoma), January 4, 1902, p. 2.

6. *Constitution of the Society of Christofolo* [sic] *Colombo of Krebs, Indian Territory.* (n.p., n.d.), p. 7.

7. *Muskogee Phoenix,* October 31, 1902, p. 1.

8. Jennings J. Rhyme, *Social and Community Problems of Oklahoma* (Guthrie: Co-operative Publishing Co.), p. 110.

9. For complete details on the Black Hand episodes in Oklahoma, see *The McAlester News-Capital,* March 31, p. 1, April 5, p. 1, and June 17, p. 1, 1909.

10. U.S. Congress, House, *Annual Report of the Secretary of Interior,* H. Ex. Doc. 1, 53rd Cong., 3rd sess., 1894, p. 143.

11. Lord, *The Italian in America,* p. 109.

12. Lieutenant J. H. Carey to Brigadier General Charles F. Barrett, November 9, 1919, Coal Strike File, Governor J. B. A. Robertson Files, Oklahoma State Archives, Oklahoma City, Oklahoma.

13. W. E. Gotcher to Edwin Dabney, February 18, 1928, Krebs Inquiry File, Governor Henry S. Johnston Files, Oklahoma State Archives, Oklahoma City, Oklahoma.

CHAPTER 5

1. Ryan, *The Rehabilitation of Oklahoma Coal Mining Communities,* p. 66.

LaVergne, TN USA
22 January 2011
213562LV00002B/7/P